Celtic Art

in cross stitch

Celtic Art

in cross stitch

BARBARA HAMMET

David & Charles

To cross stitchers everywhere, especially those who
helped so greatly by stitching projects for this book

I am particularly grateful to all the embroiderers who have helped me by stitching samples for the photographs. They are all so skillful and reliable and kindly tell me that they have enjoyed working the designs. They have done a marvellous job and I could not have managed without the help of the following people: Barbara Barnes for the Knotwork Needlework workbox lid; Jo Bostock for the La Tène tablecloth; Stephanie Bramwell for the Durrow firescreen; Margaret Burgess for the Celtic Key bookmarks; Barbara Chowienczyk for the Here Be Dragons treasure box lid; Muriel Gray for the Bird cushion and the Three Serpents picture; Joan Harris for the Greedy Cat bell-pull and the Six Serpents picture; Geoffrey Howson for the Knotwork Needlework needlecase; June Inman for a cushion for which, sadly, there was ultimately no space; Kay King for the La Tène coaster; Kate Lydford for the Celtic Key paperweight; Shirley Morris for the Figure of Eight Serpent picture; Susan Newby for the Knotwork Needlework pincushion; Llyn Parker for the Hound cushion; Valerie Ray for the Here Be Dragons picture; Carole Smith for the Peacock picture; Zoe Westwood for the Celtic Key book cover.

A DAVID & CHARLES BOOK

First published in the UK in 2002
by David & Charles
ISBN 0 7153 1213 8 (hardback)

Distributed in North America
by F&W Publications, Inc.
4700 E. Galbraith Rd.
Cincinnati, OH 45236
1-800-289-0963

Executive commissioning editor Cheryl Brown
Executive art editor Ali Myer
Book designer Lisa Forrester
Desk editor Jennifer Proverbs
Project editor Lin Clements
Photography Stewart Grant

Printed in Italy by STIGE
for David & Charles
Brunel House   Newton Abbot   Devon

Picture Credits
p7 The Board of Trinity College Dublin
p8 Cambria Archaeology, Carmarthenshire, Wales
p9 © Copyright The British Museum

contents

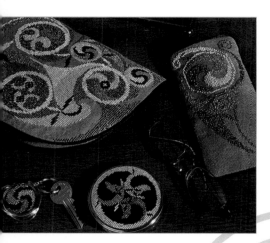

INTRODUCTION

Most people have an image in their minds of Celtic art. It may be a favourite brooch with a never-ending thread of silver weaving itself into a complex pattern, or an intricately decorated page from one of the old Gospel Books. The predominant image in most people's minds is the interlace pattern where lines weave over and under one another or themselves in sinuous curves to form elaborate geometrical patterns. Sometimes the lines turn out to be parts of an elongated creature when examined carefully enough. In the pages which follow I have used original works of Celtic art and craft as inspiration for the embroidery designs, and tried to explain something of the fascination this complex style has for me.

Many of the works I have relied on come from the great period of Celtic art from the sixth to the twelfth centuries when, in the hands of Irish Christian monks, the Celtic style reached new heights. It is the time when a tradition previously used to decorate stone and metal was released on to flat vellum and with inks and pigments flowered and flourished into something miraculously complex and intricate. But I have also looked back at the earlier Celtic style – a style with roots very far back indeed. The Celtic people (those who spoke the Celtic language) had an established culture and identity two and a half thousand years ago. Aspects of their work, their use of curves and spirals and 'S' shaped and comma motifs, are just like the ones we see in the Gospel Books.

Celtic art is a different art. To anyone brought up to revere the classical tradition, passed down through the masters of the Renaissance, it offers a distinct alternative. It is not interested in imitating outward appearances. Its love of complex, abstract pattern, curving forms and spirals seems to hint at a more mystical, fluid and flexible approach to reality.

Early Celtic Style – La Tène

In the centuries before the domination of the Roman Empire, the Celtic style known as La Tène was widespread and showed remarkable consistency from one side of Europe to the other. Unsurprisingly, the Celtic artistic tradition survived most strongly in those remote parts where Roman culture did not become established. In the years BC and for some centuries thereafter, the style was characterized by the use of wonderful curves which flow into one another and which seem at first glance abstract but which contain a multiplicity of meanings. They often appear to echo leaf or flower shapes but seem deliberately to hint at human and animal faces at the same time. A pattern can be seen as one thing, but looked at in another way, as another. Perhaps this is analogous to the shape shifting which occurs in the Celtic myths.

Celtic art often suggests flux and movement. Spiral and whirligig motifs abound. In painting and carving, plain areas contrast with ones where the intricacy of the patterns lead the eye to travel over the surface as it finds its way through intricate knots, mazes and spiral windings.

In the years before the Roman conquest, when Celtic society was pagan, the culture was an oral not a written one. What we know is pieced together from fragments written down by Greek and Roman writers who commented on their strange ways. We can also draw conclusions from the archaeological evidence. Because we are looking at a time more than 2,000 years ago, only durable materials remain, mostly metalwork and stone carving. Most of the work is non-figurative, though human heads and familiar animals and birds occur. We can see the high level of craft skill in the decoration of arms and armour, harness and chariot fittings, dishes and flagons and personal jewellery.

Symbolism

We can guess that many of the motifs used must have a magical or religious significance, probably connected with protection in battle, good luck, fertility and rites of passage into the next world. Many of the finds have been recovered from graves or from water, where it is assumed they were sacrificed. The La Tène style gets its name from the lake of that name in Switzerland where significant numbers of swords and shields were found in the nineteenth century.

From the distance of the present day it is difficult to assign meanings to objects produced by people we know so little about. Certain arrangements of shapes clearly acted as important symbols, most notably the

Manuscript painting from the Book of Kells, showing the symbols of the four evangelists (folio 129v). The man represents St Matthew, the lion St Mark, the calf St Luke and the eagle St John, all surrounded by intricate patterning.

triscele figure with three curving arms joined at the middle and radiating out. This is found so frequently that it has to be significant. In myth and art many things are represented in threes. Probably the Celtic Christians, who retained the symbol, saw it as the Trinity. Certainly the artists of the Gospel books used a complex range of symbols to add layers of extra meaning to their illustrations.

Christian Celts

It was in the hands of the Celtic Christians that the style flourished and spread. Ireland adopted Christianity as a result of the mission of St Patrick in the fifth century and it became a centre of learning and scholarship. The Christian monks were evangelical and to spread the gospel they wrote and decorated gospel books, some of which the missionaries carried far into Europe, to set up schools and monasteries. A surprising number of them have survived, a testament to the lasting quality of vellum and pigment.

The Celtic style developed over the centuries as it absorbed influences from the different cultures it came into contact with. From the Mediterranean world it encountered examples from the Roman and Coptic churches, as well as from classical antiquity. From the Picts it borrowed animal symbols and from the Saxons it learned new techniques for metalwork. Interlace ornament seems to have had a number of sources in antiquity but Celtic artists did not adopt it with enthusiasm until the seventh century. The use of elongated, interlaced animals was encouraged by contact with Anglo-Saxon culture and further elaborated under the influence of the Vikings.

Gospel Books

The Gospel book was an important innovation. The classical world was slowly adopting the 'codex' form of

Above: A Celtic cross from Nevern in Wales, richly carved all over, provides a varied source of design ideas.

Opposite: A bronze mirror in the La Tène style, from Desborough, England. The mirror back is beautifully decorated with a complex engraved pattern of curves and spirals, drawn with compasses.

book which had stitched pages, rather than the scroll, and that was the form adopted for the Gospel book. The book was composed of double pages of vellum. This was made from the skins of calves or sheep which were prepared and stretched flat and then, when inscribed, stitched together and bound. The cover was probably of tooled leather. When not placed open on the Altar, the book would be kept in an elaborate shrine of precious metal and jewels. Touching the book itself, or something it had touched, was thought to bring about miracles of healing.

The book contained the text of the four Gospels of Saints Matthew, Mark, Luke and John, and through them the life and teachings of Christ. As a record of the revealed word of God, the book was revered. Whereas classical books had been mainly text, copied by slaves, with the Gospel book the monk who wrote the text was frequently also responsible for the page decoration. To convey the glory and mystery of God to a largely illiterate world he made his book fabulously beautiful, with full pages of colourful decoration, often featuring the symbol of the Cross. These pages, called 'carpet pages', often contain detail so fine and precise that one has to agree with the comment of Gerald of Wales, who in the twelfth century inspected the Book of Kells and declared it 'the work, not of men but of angels'.

At the beginning of each Gospel, as well as a 'carpet page' of pure pattern would be another page of decoration featuring the animal that symbolized that Saint. In the Book of Durrow, one of the earliest and boldest of the books, the Saint's symbol is placed in a blank area surrounded by interlaced patterns. It has been suggested that interlaced knots entrap evil forces, thus protecting the symbols or text enclosed by them. Very early book covers used these designs, perhaps to protect the contents. An interlaced pattern was very often used where protection was important, such as at the entrances of buildings.

The beginning of the text to each Gospel would be treated to major decoration, centring on the first few letters. Those that followed gradually reduced in size and decoration. The name of God would also be decorated.

Insular Art

Irish monks developed the Celtic style of book illustration but many examples were actually made in other places, so the style is sometimes referred to as 'Insular' – of the Islands. The Irish monks founded a monastery on Iona, off the Scottish coast, and from there established centres on mainland Britain, notably at the Abbey of Lindisfarne in Northumbria, where Bishop Aedfrith wrote and decorated the superb Gospel book which survives in the British Library, though Lindisfarne was sacked by the Vikings. Iona suffered the same fate but the Book of Kells, probably created there, was ultimately carried to safety in Ireland.

Celtic Crosses

From the period of the Gospel books come the monumental stone crosses still to be seen in parts of Wales, Scotland, Ireland, Cornwall, the Isle of Man and Brittany. The cross as a symbol was not adopted by the Christian community for some centuries. One of the earliest symbols of Christianity was the 'chi rho', representing the first two letters of the Greek word for Christ. This resembled a superimposed X and a P and was surrounded by a circle representing a wreath of victory. There are examples of stone crosses with diagonal crosses (X) and others with vertical and horizontal ones – a more obvious symbol of the Cross of the crucifixion but still with the chi rho meaning as well.

The form of Celtic crosses varies from the simple early style, where a slab of stone is carved in

relief on one side, to the rather later more three-dimensional high crosses which tend to feature a cross and circle motif on a high shaft. The relief decoration on the shaft can be rich and varied including spirals, interlace, key patterns and sometimes human figures and animals. There are often similarities to the art of manuscript painting.

Metalwork

Metalwork had been a specialty of the Celtic people from the earliest times. Wonderful helmets and horse trappings, shields and scabbards, have come down to us from those times in gold, silver, bronze and iron. Brooches, bracelets, torques and hand mirrors show the variety of techniques employed. In the Christian period, these skills, and newer ones, were used to create reliquaries, bells, crosiers, chalices and crosses for the church. As with the work of the scribes, the metalworkers covered their surfaces with rich decoration and introduced a wide range of coloured effects. They used silver with black inlay for linear ornament, and enamel, coral, glass and stones to create coloured studs. For personal ornament the pennanular brooch became the dominant form. This was a highly decorated circle or broken circle attached to a pin with a decorated head – a high status jewel to fasten a cloak. The 'Tara brooch', which inspired my Here be Dragons designs, is a miracle of intricate and precise detail in the many lovely relief patterns which cover both its surfaces

My admiration for the Celtic artists has gone on growing as I have worked on this book. I hope you like some of the designs which have resulted. Perhaps because the Celtic style was so deeply ingrained in the culture of Europe, perhaps because it hints at hidden meanings, perhaps because we can all appreciate its rich abstract patterning and satisfying shapes, it is endlessly fascinating.

knotwork needlework

Original Celtic crosses can still be seen in parts of Wales, Scotland, Ireland, Cornwall and Brittany. The cross symbol, a combination of cross and circle, often tops a shaft heavily carved with interlace, key patterns, spirals and sometimes human and animal figures. The circle can be seen as a wreath or halo round the cross, perhaps the sun and the heavens or perhaps just as a line with no beginning or end – a symbol of eternity and continuity. The cross symbolizes the Crucifixion and the Tree of Life.

The cross which inspired my needlework box design was from Fahan in County Donegal, Ireland, and dates from the eighth or ninth century. I have copied the idea of an interlace of strands and cords and slightly simplified the design from the stone cross. In the original, a recessed circle links the four arms of the cross. I adapted this for a square box lid, making it more angular.

In Celtic art there are close resemblances between works in quite different media. I found the inspiration for the pincushion in the centrepiece of a full page decoration in the Gospel book, the Book of Durrow. The original forms the central circle of the fifteen, which, all closely knotted together, decorate the page. The needlecase design is another detail from the Book of Durrow, from a page dominated by a double-armed cross and filled with patterns which are variations on the cross theme. The scissor keeper is a simple entwined cross and circle.

*F*requently in Celtic art an interlaced pattern, particularly a geometric one, will be composed of strands with no beginning and no ending, as seen in these cross stitch designs.

needlework box

knotwork
needlework

DESIGN SIZE

18 x 18cm (7 x 7in) approx.

STITCH COUNT

96 x 96

MATERIALS

28 x 28cm (11 x 11in) cadet blue
14 count Aida (Zweigart code 563)

&

Stranded cotton (floss) as listed

&

Tapestry needle size 26

&

75cm (30in) braid or piping (optional)

&

Square wooden box with recess of
18.5cm (7¼in) (Market Square
Warminster Ltd, BTSQAP,
see Suppliers)

&

18 x 18cm (7 x 7in) fabric or
coloured card for inside lid

NEEDLEWORK BOX
STRANDED COTTONS

COLOUR	DMC	ANCHOR	MADEIRA	SKEINS
Gold	742	303	0107	2
Light orange	722	323	0307	1
Copper	921	1003	0311	1
Sky blue	598	167	1111	1
Darker blue	597	168	1110	1

1 Prepare your fabric and mark the centre lines with tacking (basting) (see page 107). Following the chart and using two strands of stranded cotton (floss), cross stitch out from the centre, checking your position regularly. This is a symmetrical design so you may find it tempting to turn it as you work. If you do this make sure you keep the top cross stitches in a consistent direction. Work the blue borders to finish.

2 When the embroidery is complete press the work and mount in the box lid (see page 109).

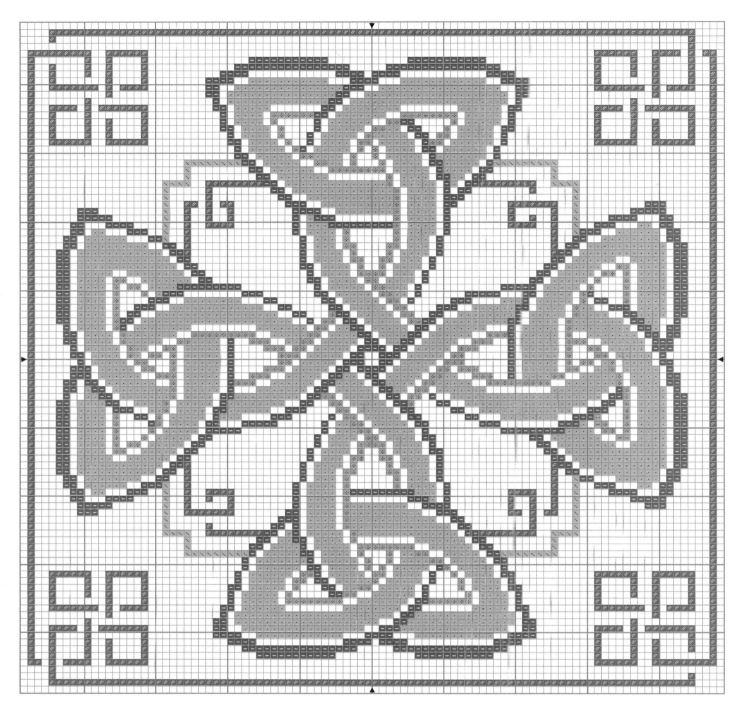

NEEDLEWORK BOX

DMC STRANDED COTTONS

·	742
⊹	722
▬	921
╲	598
⁄⁄	597

pincushion
knotwork needlework

DESIGN SIZE

12 x 12cm (4¾ x 4¾in) approx.

STITCH COUNT

67 x 67

MATERIALS

24 x 24cm (9½ x 9½in) cadet blue
14 count Aida (Zweigart code 563)

⚮

Stranded cotton (floss) as listed

⚮

Tapestry needle size 26

⚮

24 x 24cm (9½ x 9½in) backing fabric

⚮

70cm (27in) braid for edging (optional)

⚮

Polyester filling

tip

This design could be sewn on an 18 count fabric, with the border omitted, to decorate a pot lid. You could also stitch it on a 22 count Hardanger with a single strand of thread, to make a round paperweight.

COLOUR	DMC	ANCHOR	MADEIRA	SKEINS
Light orange	722	323	0307	1
Gold	742	303	0107	1
Copper	921	1003	0311	1

1 Prepare your fabric and mark the centre lines with tacking (basting) (see page 107). Follow the chart and, using two strands of stranded cotton (floss), cross stitch out from the centre, checking your position regularly. This is a symmetrical design so if you turn it as you work make sure you keep the top cross stitches in a consistent direction.

2 When the embroidery is complete press the work, then make up into a pincushion as described on page 110.

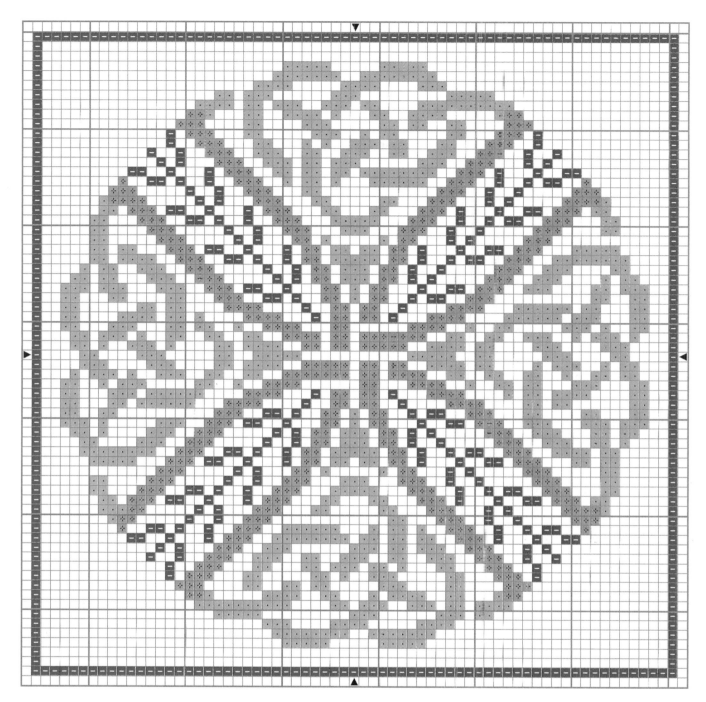

PINCUSHION
DMC STRANDED COTTONS

✛	722
•	742
▬	921

knotwork
needlecase
needlework

knotwork
needlework

NEEDLECASE
STRANDED COTTONS

COLOUR	DMC	ANCHOR	MADEIRA	SKEINS
Light orange	722	323	0307	1
Gold	742	303	0107	1
Copper	921	1003	0311	1

DESIGN SIZE

8.5 x 10.5cm (3¼ x 4¼in) approx.

STITCH COUNT

46 x 58

Finished size (folded)

9.5 x 12.5cm (3¾ x 5in)

MATERIALS

28 x 20cm (11 x 8in) cadet blue

14 count Aida (Zweigart code 563)

&

Stranded cotton (floss) as listed

&

Tapestry needle size 26

&

23 x 16.5cm (9 x 6½in) backing fabric

&

19 x 12.5cm (7½ x 5in)

iron-on interfacing

&

18 x 10cm (7 x 4in) felt for

needle 'pages'

tip

*Without the line borders above and below, this
square pattern would make an alternative
pincushion design, or could be used for a square
coaster or a greetings card.*

1 Fold the Aida in half so that the shorter ends meet and mark the fold with tacking (basting). The design is worked with the left edge of the chart against the fold. With a different colour tacking (basting) thread mark the centre horizontal. Following the chart below, begin cross stitching two blocks from the fold line using two strands of cotton (floss) throughout.

2 When the embroidery is complete press the work and then make up into a needlecase as described on page 110.

722	✦	
742	·	

NEEDLECASE
DMC STRANDED COTTONS   921   ▮

scissor keeper

DESIGN SIZE

4.5 x 4.5cm (1¾ x 1¾in) approx.

STITCH COUNT

25 x 25

MATERIALS

12 x 12cm (4½ x 4½in) cadet blue

14 count Aida (Zweigart code 563)

⚭

Stranded cotton (floss) as listed

⚭

Tapestry needle size 26

⚭

12 x 12cm (4½ x 4½in)

backing fabric

⚭

Polyester filling

SCISSOR KEEPER
STRANDED COTTONS

COLOUR	DMC	ANCHOR	MADEIRA	SKEINS
Light orange	722	323	0307	1
Gold	742	303	0107	1
Copper	921	1003	0311	1

SCISSOR KEEPER
DMC STRANDED COTTONS

722 ✛

742 ▪

921 ▬

1 Prepare your fabric and mark the centre lines with tacking (basting) (see page 107). Following the chart, cross stitch from the centre using two strands of cotton (floss). Only small quantities of thread are needed – leftovers from other projects will probably be enough.

2 When you have completed all the embroidery, remove the guide lines and press the work. Trim the fabric to 2cm (¾in) outside the embroidery and then make up into a scissor keeper as described on page 110.

tip

This neat symmetrical cross design is very quick and simple to stitch and could also be used for a bookmark or for a greetings card.

scrollwork and swirls

These designs for a handbag, mirror, spectacles case and key ring were inspired by illustrations in the Lindisfarne Gospels, written around the year 700, 'for God and for St Cuthbert' by Eadfrith, Bishop of the Lindisfarne Church. Many sorts of decoration are included in this richly illustrated manuscript, but for the handbag I selected a part of the initial page to the Gospel of St Luke which concentrates on the dynamic spirals and trumpet shapes which have been an enduring feature of Celtic art since pagan times. The design is based on half the infilling pattern of the initial letter Q. I liked the asymmetry which I felt emphasized the rhythmic flow from one area to another. The designs in the three dominant circles act almost like cogwheels, stirring the whole surface into movement. In the manuscript the design is green, blue, red, orange, yellow and black but I have altered this to a more subtle colouring.

The mirror is a detail from the same design but on black Aida, contrasted with metallic and shiny rayon threads. The concave and convex curves, arranged to form a triscele motif, can be seen as an abstract design or as three birds' heads. The spectacle case is based on a detail from another area of the same manuscript page. The motifs are very similar to those on the bag, including the smaller circle which is divided by an 'S' shape into yin/yang divisions. A striking key ring repeats the triscele theme.

The threads and fabrics used in these projects reflect the colours and textures of rocky landscape – stone, flint, sand, earth, copper and lead. Stranded cotton and metallic threads combine with rayon floss on Cashel linen and black Aida.

handbag

SCROLLWORK AND SWIRLS

DESIGN SIZE

23 x 18cm (9 x 7in) approx.

STITCH COUNT

125 x 100

MATERIALS

51 x 36cm (20 x 14in) grey 28
count Cashel linen (Zweigart code
781) or flint 14 count Aida (Fabric
Flair N14.781)

&

DMC stranded cotton (floss),
metallic stranded thread and
rayon floss as listed

&

Tapestry needle size 24

&

28 x 23cm (11 x 9in) grey 28 count
Cashel linen or alternative
for making the front of the bag

&

Two pieces of lining material
28 x 41cm (11 x 16in) and
28 x 23cm (11 x 9in)

&

Firm iron-on interfacing

&

Piping cord to finish edges (optional)

&

Sewing thread to match

HANDBAG		
COLOUR		SKEINS
DMC STRANDED COTTONS		
Sand	437	1
Black	310	1
DMC METALLIC STRANDED		
Copper	5279	2
Dark silver	5287	2
Silver	5283	1
DMC RAYON FLOSS		
Shiny sand	30738	1
Earth	30898	2
Stone	30739	1

1 Read through the instructions before you begin. Select the larger piece of linen which forms the front flap and back of your bag. (Note: the linen texture looks good but Aida would be easier to work.) Fold the fabric in half so that it measures 25.5 x 36cm (10 x 14in). Measure down 9cm (3½in) from the fold and mark with tacking (basting) what will be the central horizontal guide line for the area to be embroidered. Fold the fabric the other way and mark a vertical guide line, bisecting the first. Press the fabric and mount on an embroidery frame.

2 Following the charts on pages 22–23, begin cross stitching near the centre of the design, counting carefully. Use two strands over two threads of evenweave throughout (see page 106 for using rayon floss and metallic stranded threads). When the embroidery is complete remove the guide lines and press.

3 Mark out the shape of the pieces ready to make up the bag by making a template from the shape of the flap –

follow the instructions given with the diagrams (right).

4 Press interfacing to the wrong side of the embroidered fabric for the flap and the back, and the piece of fabric which is to make the front of the bag.

5 If you want to add piping cord, position it now on the right side of the larger piece, with the piping facing inwards, so that the stitching line follows the stitching line in the diagram. Tack (baste) the piping in place all round.

6 Tack (baste) the embroidered fabric and lining fabric right sides together around the outside of the flap, following the stitching line shown on the diagram around the shaded half. Stitch through all thicknesses. Turn the bag over so the wrong side of the lining is facing up. Fold the unstitched part of the lining out of the way.

7 Now take the fabric for the front of the bag. Fold in the seam allowance along the top edge and press the fold. Place the front section, with the right

side down, on top of the area for the back of the bag, so that the fold touches the edge of the flap embroidery. Stitch carefully together, following the stitching line you marked out.

8 Turn the bag over and fold back the front and back sections you have just stitched together. Take the front piece of the lining and repeat step 7. Stitch slightly inside the marked line to help the lining fit neatly inside the outer.

9 You should now have a lined embroidered flap with an embroidery fabric bag and a lining fabric bag attached to it with the openings facing each other. Trim the seam allowance about 0.5cm (¼in) from the stitching and turn right side out. Tuck the lining into the main bag so the folded and pressed

edges meet. Stitch together by hand. Press the finished bag carefully, doing the flap from the lined side.

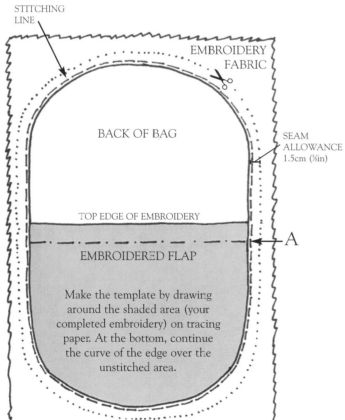

How to prepare the pieces for making up the bag.
Fold the template over at point A, 2cm (¾in) from the top edge of the embroidery (see diagram, left). Use the resulting folded template as a guide to the shape of the bag back and the bag front. Remember to add a seam allowance of 1.5cm (⅝in) before cutting out. Cut identical pieces from your chosen lining fabric.

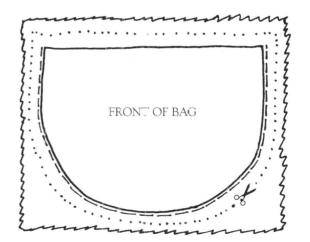

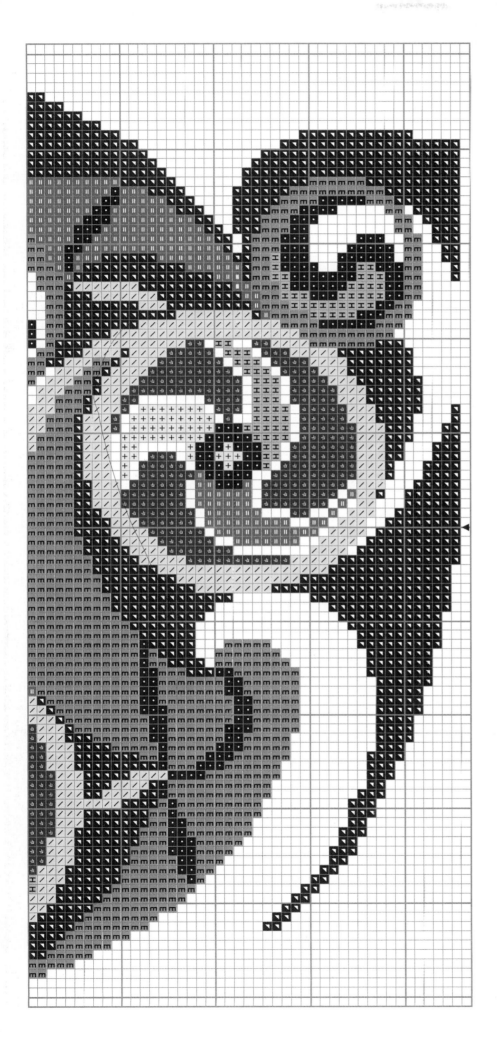

HANDBAG

DMC STRANDED COTTONS

m	437
■	310

DMC METALLIC THREAD

II	5279
⅃	5287
+	5283

DMC RAYON FLOSS

I	30738
◣	30898
/	30739

handbag mirror

DESIGN SIZE

6.5 x 6.5cm (2½ x 2½in) approx.

STITCH COUNT

47 x 48

MATERIALS

15 x 15cm (6 x 6in) black
18 count Aida

&

DMC metallic stranded thread and
rayon floss as listed

&

Tapestry needle size 26

&

Iron-on interfacing

&

Handbag mirror (Framecraft, code
HBM3, see Suppliers)

1 Prepare your fabric and mark the centre lines with tacking (basting) (see page 107). Following the chart, cross stitch the design using one strand of rayon floss and one of metallic stranded (see page 106 for advice on using rayon floss and metallic threads).

2 Once all the stitching is complete, iron the fusible interfacing on to the reverse of the embroidery. To mount in the mirror, check the appearance by standing the gilt ring from the mirror kit over the design to check that the stitching fills the space. Mark the position with pins. Position the template from the mirror kit over the interfacing side, draw round it then carefully cut a circle around the design. Assemble according to the manufacturer's instructions.

HANDBAG MIRROR		
COLOUR		SKEINS
DMC METALLIC STRANDED		
Copper	5279	1
Silver	5283	1
DMC RAYON FLOSS		
Pearl grey	30414	1
Stone	30739	1

HANDBAG MIRROR

DMC METALLIC STRANDED

5279 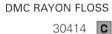 II

5283 +

DMC RAYON FLOSS

30414 C

30739 /

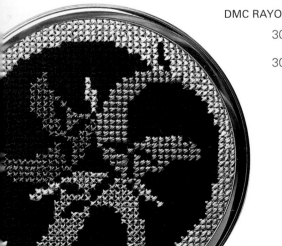

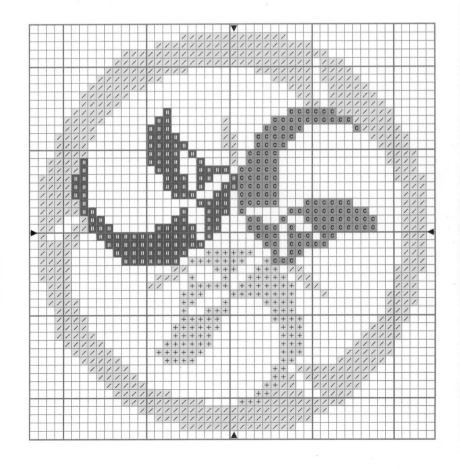

key ring

DESIGN SIZE

2.75 x 2.75cm (1 x 1in) approx.

STITCH COUNT

20 x 20

MATERIALS

10 x 10cm (4 x 4in) black
18 count Aida

&

DMC metallic stranded thread and
rayon floss as listed

&

Tapestry needle size 26

&

Iron-on interfacing

&

Key ring (Framecraft,
code KF3, see Suppliers)

KEY RING		
COLOUR		SKEINS
DMC METALLIC STRANDED		
Copper	5279	1
Silver	5283	1
DMC RAYON FLOSS		
Pearl grey	30414	1

1 Find the centre of the fabric and cross stitch from here, following the chart and using one strand of rayon floss and one of metallic stranded thread (see page 106 for using rayon floss and metallic stranded threads).

2 When the stitching is complete, iron the fusible interfacing on to the back of the embroidery. Position the template from the key ring over the interfacing side. Draw around it and carefully cut a circle round the design. Now assemble in the key ring according to the manufacturer's instructions.

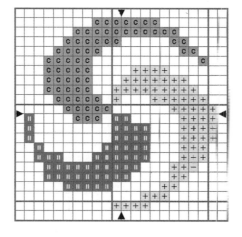

KEY RING

DMC METALLIC STRANDED

5279 ▥

5283 ＋

DMC RAYON FLOSS

30414 C

spectacles case

DESIGN SIZE

8 x 16.5cm (3¼ x 6½in) approx.

STITCH COUNT

43 x 90

MATERIALS

19 x 28cm (7½ x 11in)
grey 28 count Cashel linen
(Zweigart code 781)

⚬

DMC metallic stranded thread and
rayon floss as listed

⚬

Tapestry needle size 26

⚬

Iron-on interfacing

⚬

13 x 23cm (5 x 9in) grey 28 count
Cashel linen for the backing

⚬

13 x 38cm (5 x 15in) lining fabric,
perhaps quilted

⚬

Cord to finish (optional)

SPECTACLES CASE		
COLOUR		SKEINS
DMC METALLIC STRANDED		
Copper	5279	1
Dark silver	5287	1
Silver	5283	1
DMC RAYON FLOSS		
Pearl grey	30414	1

1 Prepare the larger piece of linen by marking the central vertical and horizontal lines with tacking (basting) (see page 107). (Alternatively, you could use a 14 count Aida in flint, Fabric Flair N14.781.) Mount the fabric on a frame to prevent distortion.

2 Following the chart, cross stitch using two strands of rayon floss and two of metallic stranded thread (see page 106 for advice on using these threads).

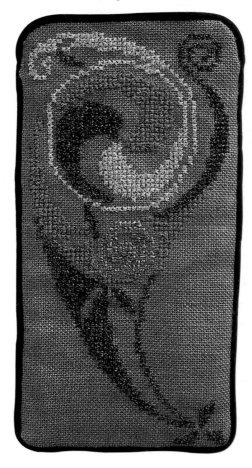

3 Check for omissions and press, then iron the iron-on interfacing to the reverse of the embroidery and to the piece of linen for the back.

4 Fold the top of the embroidered piece over, two threads above the top stitches and press from the back. Turn over 2cm (¾in) on the other linen piece and press. Place the two pieces right sides together and pin together at the sides close to the stitching. At the bottom, pin together two threads below the embroidery. Stitch together, leaving the top open, trim the seams and turn right side out.

5 Fold the lining fabric in half with right sides together. Turn over the fabric at the top so that the lining will be marginally shorter than the outer piece, then press. Stitch together at the sides so that it will fit inside the outer piece. Trim the seams. Place inside the outer piece and stitch together invisibly using ladder stitch (see page 108) to complete.

6 If adding decorative cord, tuck one end in between the embroidery and the lining at the front and stitch all around the edge of the case with invisible stitches. Stitch across the back and secure inside to finish.

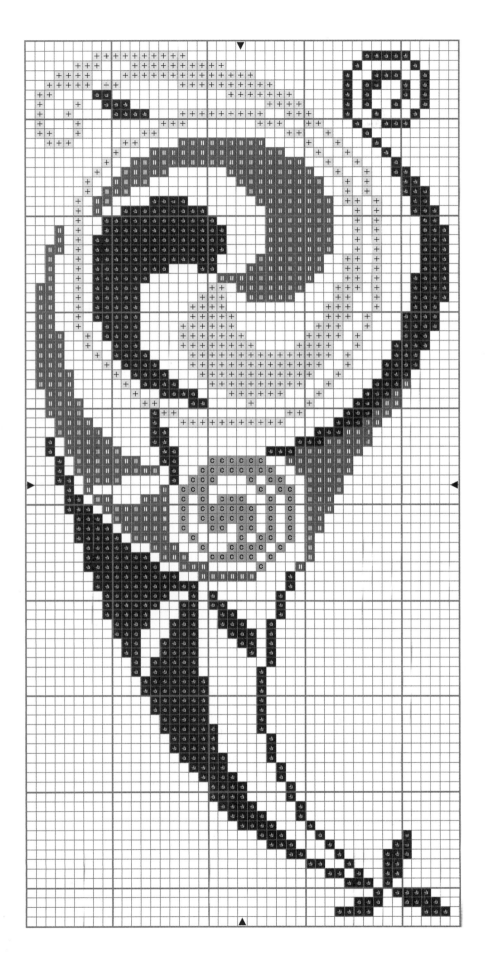

SPECTACLES CASE

DMC METALLIC STRANDED

| ‖ | 5279 |
| 5287 |
| + | 5283 |

DMC RAYON FLOSS

| C | 30414 |

book of kells peacock picture

The Book of Kells, a magnificent, lavishly illustrated Gospel manuscript from around 800 AD, is so complex that I have selected just a detail from one of the pages as inspiration for this picture. The page, folio 32v, is a full-length portrait of Christ, flanked by peacocks and angels, surrounded by bands of complex interwoven birds and animals.

I had to be very selective and chose the peacocks and the chalice sprouting vines as the main elements, moving the chalice and vine from beneath the peacocks' feet to fill the central space. Highly decorative in their own right, the peacocks symbolized immortality, their flesh considered incorruptible. In their relationship with the chalice sprouting vines they represent the resurrection of Christ. This meaning is emphasized by the circular motifs with red crosses on the wings, which represent Eucharist wafers.

Unusually, this particular page of the Book of Kells has empty spaces in the top corners above the semicircular arch, so I borrowed from another page with a similar format, showing St Matthew. From this came the mauve colouring and the spreading decoration. This represents the flabellum, a sort of fan used in the early church to keep the altar clear of flies. It came to signify purification and is often shown in the hands of angels.

I could not find a pleasing fabric in the original colour range but incorporating the mauve colouring for the top corners suggested the delicate mauvey-pink colour of the fabric eventually selected.

This picture was inspired by the complex imagery of the Book of Kells. It can be appreciated for its decorative qualities or, on a symbolic level, as a representation of eternal life.

peacock picture

book of kells
peacock picture

DESIGN SIZE

42 x 26cm (16½ x 10½in) approx.

STITCH COUNT

231 x 144

MATERIALS

53 x 38cm (21 x 15in) English rose
28 count Jobelan
(Fabric Flair FQ429.167)

&

Stranded cotton (floss) as listed

&

Tapestry needle size 26

PEACOCK PICTURE
STRANDED COTTONS

COLOUR	DMC	ANCHOR	MADEIRA	SKEINS
Black	310	403	black	2
Antique violet	3041	871	0806	2
Grape	3835	98	0809	1
Dark purple	154	897	0811	1
Golden yellow	728	306	0114	2
Cream	3823	386	0101	1
Light straw	677	886	2207	1
Light yellow	744	301	0110	1
Old gold	783	307	2211	1
Dark old gold	782	901	2212	1
Fudge	977	1002	2307	1
Bright jade	958	187	1114	1
Darker jade	943	188	1203	1
Bright turquoise	3843	410	1009	1
Dark turquoise	3808	170	1108	1
Blue	825	162	1011	1
Dark navy blue	336	149	1007	1
Sea blue	807	168	1108	1
Red	817	46	0211	1
Coral	351	10	0214	1
Copper	920	1004	0312	1
Apricot	722	323	0307	1
Light grey green	3813	875	1702	1
Darker grey green	502	876	1703	1

1 Prepare your fabric and mark the centre vertical and horizontal lines with tacking (basting) (see page 107). It would also be helpful to mark a grid with tacking (basting) stitches every forty threads (twenty stitches), counting out from the centre lines. Mount the fabric on an embroidery frame to prevent distortion.

2 Following the charts on pages 31–33, begin cross stitching just below the centre of the design, using two strands of stranded cotton (floss) over two threads of fabric throughout. Work the chalice with grape vine and then count out to establish the placing of the two peacocks. Embroider the peacocks, checking their

positions carefully. Leave the black backstitch lines until last.

3 Work the outline of the semicircular archway with black stranded cotton (floss), first the inner then the outer line. Work the outlines of the rectangular outer border.

4 Embroider the gold-coloured bands now. These are gold leaf in the original which has worn to create a broken, antique effect. If you make minor errors in placing the different gold colours it will not matter too much because it will still give the desired effect. Finally, work the decorative patterns in the top corners before filling in with the antique violet colour.

5 When the embroidery is complete remove the guide lines and press the work and frame as a picture (see page 108 for advice). The picture shown has been framed with a narrow margin of fabric showing around the edge.

310 ▯
3041 ⊻
3835 ⊽
154 ⌄
728 ⚲
3823 ◿
677 ⦂
744 ⤬
783 ⫽
782 ▽
977 ◪
958 T
943 ╋
3843 ⬤
3808 ⊞
825 ⬃
336 ◉
807 ⟍
817 ⌐
351 ✕
920 C
722 ∩
3813 ▬
502 ═

Backstitch in
black 310
▬▬

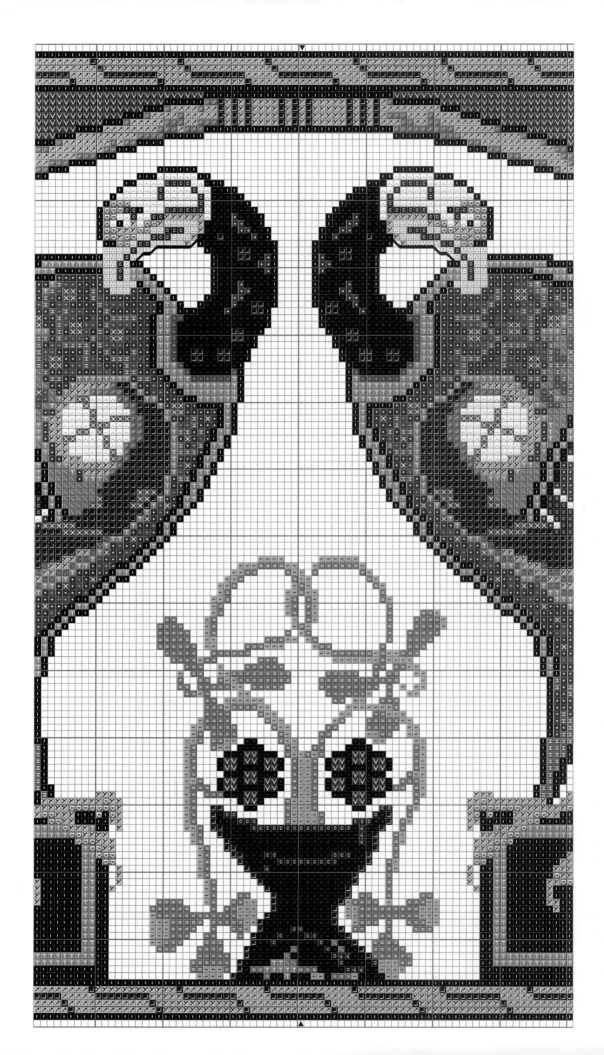

▮	310
⍌	3041
▼	3835
⌄	154
➚	728
⌂	3823
⛶	677
⛝	744
⫽	783
▽	782
⧄	977
T	958
+	943
●	3843
⊟	3808
◺	825
○	336
╲	807
⌐	817
✕	351
⋂	722
▬	3813
═	502

Backstitch in
black 310
━━━

celtic key

All of the items in this section are decorated with Celtic key patterns – arresting images worked in a striking colour scheme. These patterns, sometimes described as Celtic fret patterns, are characteristic of Celtic Christian art, occurring in manuscript painting and in carved stone crosses. I have isolated the key patterns and used them as the entire decoration but in Celtic art they were always used as one element in a complex arrangement.

The pot lid and card use the same basic design, an angular version of an 'S' scroll, repeated. Each 'S' interlinks with the next leaving a gap the same width as the stitched design. This creates an ambiguity as the eye wonders whether to follow the 'positive' path of the stitching or the 'negative' path of the fabric. Unlike the Christian mazes in the floors of cathedrals like Chartres, there is no beginning and end after a long journey, but many possibilities. These Celtic key patterns were used on the diagonal, unlike the Greek key patterns from which they may derive. The bowl lid, which is circular, is charted and worked on the straight for convenience.

The notebook cover and paperweight designs feature a single line which both defines a shape and fills it with pattern. They are derived from carved stone crosses found in Wales. The bookmarks follow a similar idea. The bolder one, from the Canterbury Psalter, uses the stitched line to define and decorate. The other bookmark is more delicate and it is the 'negative' space, the linen fabric, which defines the shape and fills it with a fretwork pattern, providing alternative routes round.

Celtic key patterns have a maze-like fascination as our eyes seem compelled to follow the paths as they twist and turn into elaborate geometric patterns, as seen in this book cover, paperweight, bookmarks, trinket bowl and card.

notebook cover

NOTEBOOK COVER
STRANDED COTTON

COLOUR	DMC	ANCHOR	MADEIRA	SKEINS
Copper red	920	1004	0312	2

DESIGN SIZE

9.25 x 14cm (3¾ x 5½in) approx.

STITCH COUNT

51 x 77

MATERIALS

48 x 24cm (19 x 9½in) black 14 count Aida or 28 count evenweave

⚬

Stranded cotton (floss) as listed

⚬

Tapestry needle size 26

⚬

42 x 16cm (16½ x 6¼in) iron-on interfacing

⚬

A6 notebook

1 Prepare the embroidery fabric by folding the long side in half. With the fold on the left, mark a line with tacking (basting) stitches 1.25cm (½in) from the fold. This marks the left edge of the design. Find the centre of the shorter side and mark a horizontal guide line with tacking (basting).

2 Following the chart, begin cross stitching from the left side using two strands of stranded cotton (floss). Work a square block at a time.

3 When the embroidery is complete remove the guide lines and press the work. The embroidery can now be used to cover a book – see instructions on page 109.

NOTEBOOK COVER
DMC STRANDED COTTON

920 ■

paperweight

celtic key

DESIGN SIZE

7 x 7cm (2¾ x 2¾in) approx.

STITCH COUNT

51 x 51

MATERIALS

15 x 15cm (6 x 6in) black
18 count Aida

⚭

Stranded cotton (floss) as listed

⚭

Tapestry needle size 26

⚭

8 x 8cm (3 x 3in) iron-on
interfacing

⚭

46 x 19cm (18 x 7½in)
backing fabric

⚭

Round glass paperweight
(Framecraft, code PW3,
see Suppliers)

⚭

Black sticky-backed felt to replace
green in paperweight

PAPERWEIGHT
STRANDED COTTON

COLOUR	DMC	ANCHOR	MADEIRA	SKEINS
Copper red	920	1004	0312	1

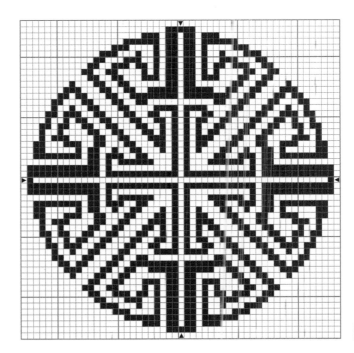

PAPERWEIGHT
DMC STRANDED COTTON

■ 920

1 Prepare your fabric and mark the centre lines with tacking (basting) (see page 107). Following the chart, begin cross stitching from the centre using one strand of stranded cotton (floss) throughout.

2 When the embroidery is complete remove the guide lines and press. Iron the interfacing on to the back of the embroidery. Using the template provided with the paperweight, carefully cut out a circle to fit in the paperweight and then assemble according to the manufacturer's instructions. Stick the black sticky-backed felt to the underside of the paperweight.

bowl lid

celtic key

BOWL LID
STRANDED COTTON

COLOUR	DMC	ANCHOR	MADEIRA	SKEINS
Copper red	920	1004	0312	1

DESIGN SIZE

9 x 9cm (3½ x 3½in) approx.

STITCH COUNT

57 x 59

MATERIALS

18 x 18cm (7 x 7in) black
16 count Aida

&

Stranded cotton (floss) as listed

&

Tapestry needle size 26

&

10 x 10cm (4 x 4in)
iron-on interfacing

&

Wooden bowl with lid (Framecraft,
code W4R, see Suppliers)

BOWL LID
DMC STRANDED COTTON

■ 920

1 Prepare your fabric and mark the centre lines with tacking (basting) (see page 107). Following the chart, begin cross stitching from the centre using one strand of stranded cotton (floss).

2 When the embroidery is complete remove the guide lines and press. Iron the interfacing on to the back of the embroidery. Using the template provided with the bowl, carefully cut out a circle to fit in the lid and assemble according to the manufacturer's instructions.

card celtic key

CARD
STRANDED COTTON

COLOUR	DMC	ANCHOR	MADEIRA	SKEINS
Copper red	920	1004	0312	1

DESIGN SIZE

6.75 x 7cm (2½ x 2¾in) approx.

STITCH COUNT

37 x 40

MATERIALS

10 x 15cm (4 x 6in) black
14 count Aida

&

Stranded cotton (floss) as listed

&

Tapestry needle size 26

&

10 x 15cm (4 x 6in) fusible
interfacing

&

Greetings card with 8cm (3in)
aperture (Craft Creations, code
DE10U cream, see Suppliers)

&

Double-sided adhesive tape

1 Prepare your fabric and mark the centre lines with tacking (basting) (see page 107). Following the chart, begin cross stitching from the centre using two strands of stranded cotton (floss) throughout.

2 When the embroidery is complete remove the guide lines and press the work. Iron the interfacing on to the back of the embroidery. Mount in the card using double-sided adhesive tape along the top.

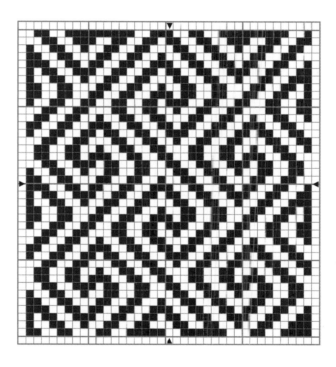

CARD
DMC STRANDED COTTON

■ 920

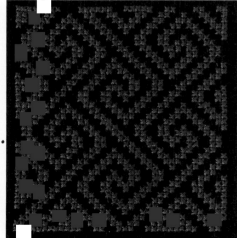

tip

This repeated pattern is a very useful one as not only is it simple and quick to stitch, but it can also be continued to fill any shape or size, or be used as a border around a central design.

bookmarks

celtic key

BOOKMARKS
STRANDED COTTONS

COLOUR	DMC	ANCHOR	MADEIRA	SKEINS
Copper red	920	1004	0312	1
Black	310	403	black	1

▨ BOLD BOOKMARK ▨

DESIGN SIZE

4 x 19cm (1½ x 7½in) approx.

STITCH COUNT

22 x 105

▨ DELICATE BOOKMARK ▨

DESIGN SIZE

4.5 x 19cm (1¾ x 7½in) approx.

STITCH COUNT

24 x 105

MATERIALS

(for each bookmark)

30cm (12in) natural, 28 count evenweave linen band (Zweigart code 7311, colour 53)

⚬

Stranded cotton (floss) as listed

⚬

Tapestry needle size 26

⚬

25 x 4.5cm (10 x 1¾in) backing fabric or felt

1 Prepare your fabric and mark the centre lines with tacking (basting) (see page 107). Following the chart, begin stitching from the centre at the edge, using two strands of stranded cotton (floss) over two threads of linen throughout. The bold bookmark begins two threads from the edge while the delicate one starts close to the edging.

2 When the embroidery is complete remove the guide lines. Fold over the ends so that each bookmark measures about 22cm (8¾in) and press the folds. Trim the surplus back to 2cm (¾in) and fold in the scalloped edging of the turning.

3 Fold and trim the backing fabric so that it is 1.25cm (½in) shorter than the bookmark, then hand sew in place.

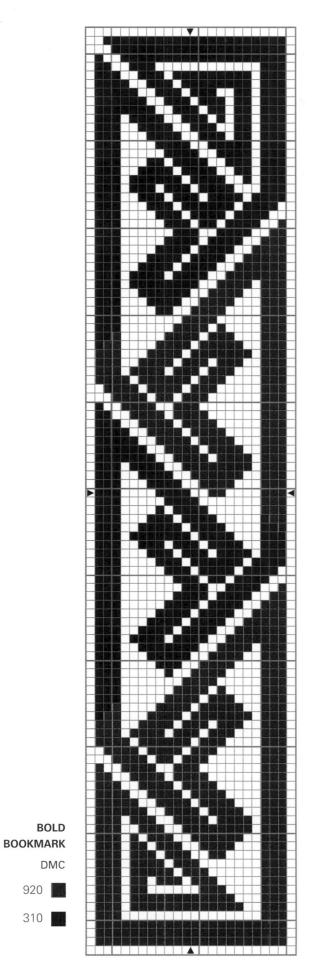

**BOLD
BOOKMARK**

DMC

920 ■

310 ■

**DELICATE
BOOKMARK**

DMC

■ 920

■ 310

here be dragons

These designs were inspired by the Tara brooch, discovered in 1850 by two Irish children near the ancient Irish royal town of Tara. It is a richly decorated penannular brooch from the early eighth century, a masterpiece of intricate design, demonstrating a wealth of craft techniques. The ornament, covering front and back, includes interlaced beasts and birds, areas of spiral decoration and borders of curvilinear patterns. The effect is very rich and textural, reflecting light from a variety of shiny surfaces.

I have tried to capture this effect by using the sheen of variously coloured rayon floss and the glitter of fine metallic braids, while the light and dark shades used try to capture the interplay of light and shade. The dragon-like beasts selected for the picture are from the front of the Tara brooch, their ears and tails, as well as their sinuous, serpent-like bodies, forming the essential interlaced elements. The pattern used at the base comes from the outer edge of the brooch and is in a technique which makes it appear to be made up from lines of tiny gold beads, hence the variety of threads used. The top corners of the design are taken from the reverse of the brooch, an area in silver inlaid with a black design.

The attractive trinket box features the two animals which dominate the back of the Tara brooch. Their bodies bend into the spiral shapes which Celtic artists loved and their fierce heads, limbs and tails all interlace. The copper shapes knot themselves decoratively to fill the remaining space.

Fierce golden dragons on a dark fabric make an unusual picture and also twine together to decorate the lid of a box, guarding your gold trinkets.

tara dragons picture

here be dragons

here be dragons

DESIGN SIZE

34.5 x 14cm (13½ x 5½in) approx.

STITCH COUNT

189 x 78

MATERIALS

46 x 28cm (18 x 11in) black
14 count Aida or a 28 count
evenweave, like Quaker cloth

⚭

DMC rayon floss and Kreinik
Fine (#8) metallic braids as listed

⚭

Tapestry needle size 26

1 Prepare your fabric and mark the centre lines with tacking (basting) (see page 107). Cross stitch the design using two strands of rayon floss and one strand of Kreinik Fine (#8) Braid over one block of Aida or two threads of evenweave. See page 106 for stitching with rayon floss and metallic threads.

2 Following the chart, stitch out from the centre, beginning with the twisted band which separates the dragon segments. Keep checking your position carefully. I would suggest working the vertical and horizontal parts of the frames around the dragons next.

3 When the embroidery is complete press the work, taking care with the rayon and metallic threads. Mount and frame with a margin of black fabric all round the embroidery of about 3.75cm (1½in). A frame with an aperture of about 42 x 22cm (16½ x 8½in) will be required (see page 108 for framing).

TARA DRAGONS PICTURE

COLOUR		REELS
KREINIK FINE (#8) BRAID		
Bright gold	002HL	2
Vatican gold	102HL	1
Aztec gold	202HL	1
Copper	021HL	1

DMC RAYON FLOSS		SKEINS
Sun gold	30972	2
Honey gold	30726	1
Light gold	30745	1
Autumn gold	30976	1
Shadow gold	30301	1
Silver grey	30762	1
Grey	30415	2

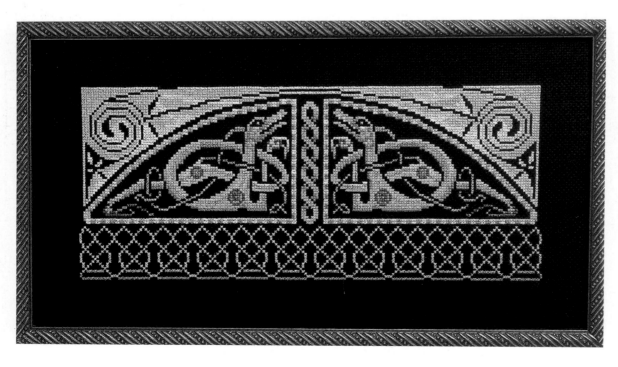

TARA DRAGONS PICTURE

KREINIK FINE (#8) BRAID

Code	Symbol
002HL	c
102HL	>
202HL	‖
021HL	=

DMC RAYON FLOSS

Code	Symbol
30972	+
30726	×
30745	≈
30976	V
30301	↙
30762	»
30415	⋇

TARA DRAGONS PICTURE

Symbol	Thread
KREINIK FINE (#8) BRAID	
C	002HL
∧	102HL
=	202HL
‖	021HL
DMC RAYON FLOSS	
+	30972
×	30726
2	30745
▷	30976
◣	30301
≫	30762
✕	30415

dragons box

DESIGN SIZE

10.5 x 15cm (4 x 6in) approx.

STITCH COUNT

58 x 82

MATERIALS

46 x 28cm (18 x 11in) black 14
count Aida or 28 count evenweave

☙

DMC rayon floss and Kreinik Fine
(#8) metallic braids as listed in
chart key (1 reel or skein of each)

☙

Tapestry needle size 26

☙

Trinket box to fit design (Market
Square Warminster Ltd, code
BTMNP, see Suppliers)

☙

Metallic cord to edge (optional)

1 Prepare your fabric and mark the
centre lines. Cross stitch from the centre
using two strands of rayon floss and one
strand of Fine (#8) Braid over one block
of Aida or two threads of evenweave.

2 Press the embroidery. The pine box
shown is treated with a black stain and
clear varnish. To mount the work in the
lid, follow the instructions on page 109,
edging with gold cord if desired.

DRAGONS BOX

DMC RAYON FLOSS		KREINIK FINE (#8) BRAID	
+	30972	C	002HL
×	30726	>	102HL
~	30745	‖	202HL
V	30976	=	021HL
◿	30301		

circular serpents

Serpents are a recurrent motif in the Book of Kells. Their long, simple bodies, prominent heads and eyes and often fish-like tails, lend themselves to being twisted into letter shapes or to filling areas with complex interlaced patterns. Symbolically, serpents played a role in early Celtic art, associated with the mother goddess, life, fertility and regeneration. In the Book of Kells they were reinterpreted in Christian iconography. Biblically the serpent was evil, tempting mankind to sin. It also represented eternal life because shedding its skin was thought to rejuvenate it. Celtic artists seemed to love ambiguity.

For these embroideries I have selected four very small details from the manuscript, inspired by folio 29r, a page where four touching roundels are at the top of one of the designs. Two of them contain serpent motifs, one with six and one with three. Nearby is the design I used to make the Figure of Eight embroidery, featuring four serpents. From another page I selected the design of four serpents dividing the circle into quarters.

The mauve-pinks and blues are not the actual colours of the original, in which the serpents tend to be monochrome. It seemed reasonable to bring some of the rich colours around them into the circles of snakes. In all four designs, the main interlace patterns are created by the serpents' bodies. The subsidiary dark pink lines which weave in and out are continuations of the eye features. Only in the Figure of Eight design is the pink line a continuous, separate entity.

These four designs demonstrate the Celtic feeling for structure and geometrical pattern, as always, expressed through curving lines.

circular serpents pictures

MATERIALS
(for each of the four designs)

28 x 28cm (11 x 11in)
Confederate grey 16 count Aida
(Zweigart code 718) or 32 count
evenweave Belfast linen

⚭

Stranded cotton (floss) as listed

⚭

Tapestry needle size 26

⚭

20cm (8in) diameter wooden
frame (Turnstyle Crafted Wooden
Products, code 004, see
Suppliers)

⚭

Mount board

quarters picture

DESIGN SIZE
17 x 17cm (6¾ x 6¾in) approx.

STITCH COUNT
108 x 108

figure of eight picture

DESIGN SIZE
17 x 17cm (6¾ x 6¾in) approx.

STITCH COUNT
109 x 109

**QUARTERS AND
FIGURE OF EIGHT PICTURE**
STRANDED COTTONS

COLOUR	DMC	ANCHOR	MADEIRA	SKEINS
Black	310	403	black	1
Plum pink	3803	69	0602	1
Strong blue	3842	164	1010	1
Cream	746	386	0101	1
Pink	316	1017	0809	1
Pale pink	778	1016	2610	1
Pale antique violet	3042	870	0807	1
Antique violet	3041	871	0806	1
Light blue	3766	1038	1110	1
Light turquoise	959	185	1113	1

three serpents picture

DESIGN SIZE

17 x 17cm (6¾ x 6¾in) approx.

STITCH COUNT

107 x 107

TO WORK ALL FOUR DESIGNS

1   Prepare your fabric and mark the centre lines with tacking (basting) (see page 107). Please note, these designs were embroidered using DMC threads; the alternatives given in the thread lists may not always be exactly the same.

2   Following the charts, cross stitch each design from the centre using two strands of stranded cotton (floss) over one block of Aida or two threads of evenweave. Work the black outlines first, and next work the plum pink. Then go on to fill in the colours of the serpents. When the embroidery is complete press the work carefully.

3   Cut a 21.5cm (8½in) diameter circle of mount board to fit inside your frame. Place the embroidery face down and place the card circle in position so that the embroidery is in its centre. Work a line of running stitches 0.5cm (¼in) outside the edge. Draw the stitches up around the board. If necessary, to produce a neat result, work an extra row of running stitches a little way from the first. When you are satisfied with the appearance (check it from the front) you can trim away the excess fabric. It is now ready to frame.

six serpents picture

DESIGN SIZE

17 x 17cm (6¾ x 6¾in) approx.

STITCH COUNT

108 x 109

THREE SERPENTS PICTURE
STRANDED COTTONS

COLOUR	DMC	ANCHOR	MADEIRA	SKEINS
Black	310	403	black	1
Plum pink	3803	69	0602	1
Strong blue	3842	164	101C	1
Cream	746	386	0101	1
Pink	316	1017	0809	1
Pale pink	778	1016	2610	1
Pale antique violet	3042	870	0807	1
Light blue	3766	1038	1110	1

SIX SERPENTS PICTURE
STRANDED COTTONS

COLOUR	DMC	ANCHOR	MADEIRA	SKEINS
Black	310	403	black	1
Plum pink	3803	69	0602	1
Strong blue	3842	164	1010	1
Cream	746	386	0101	1
Pink	316	1017	0809	1
Pale pink	778	1016	2610	1
Pale violet	153	95	0802	1
Pale antique violet	3042	870	0807	1
Light blue	3766	1038	1110	1
Light turquoise	959	185	1113	1

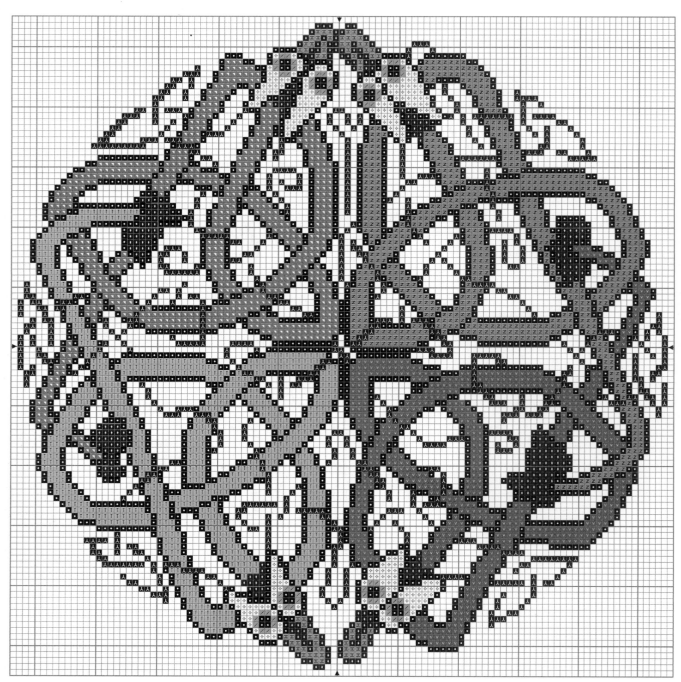

QUARTERS PICTURE
DMC STRANDED COTTONS

■ 310		╱ 778	
⅄ 3803		I 3042	
◆ 3842		V 3041	
⊹ 746		T 3766	
◣ 316		Z 959	

FIGURE OF EIGHT PICTURE

DMC STRANDED COTTONS

■	310	╱	778
↗	3803	⊥	3042
◆	3842	v	3041
⊡	746	⊤	3766
◥	316	z	959

THREE SERPENTS PICTURE
DMC STRANDED COTTONS

⬢	310	◣	316
人	3803	╱	778
◆	3842	⊥	3042
⊹	746	T	3766

SIX SERPENTS PICTURE
DMC STRANDED COTTONS

■	310	⁄	778
人	3803	◇	153
◆	3842	エ	3042
✛	746	⊤	3766
◣	316	Z	959

durrow circle firescreen

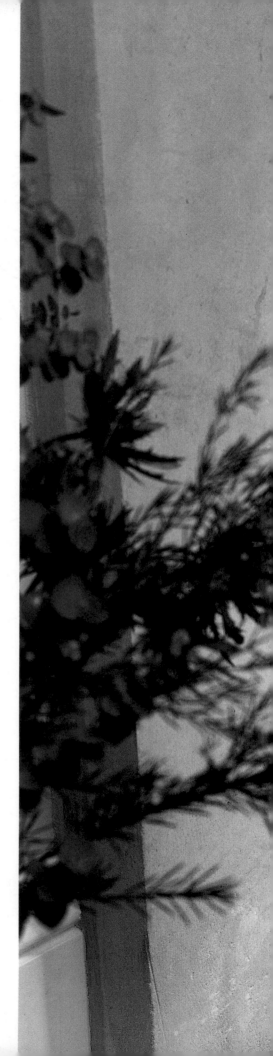

This design has all the qualities I admire in Celtic art: the curves, the spirals, the interweaving, the complexity, the abstract geometry, and the sense of movement as the eye follows the ribbons of colour. The embroidery was inspired by the decorated pages of the Book of Durrow, one of the earlier Gospel books (dating probably from the late seventh century). It is characterized by its strikingly bold style and colouring.

The circular design, set in a square frame, is taken from a carpet page where it is surrounded by six panels of entwined, curvy animals. I found the two simpler bands for the top and bottom in the borders of other pages. It is a characteristic of the Book of Durrow that the bands which form the patterns are continuous but change colour, drawing attention to different aspects of the design. In the firescreen the use of red and gold in the central disc reminds us that threes are central to Celtic art, whilst the green used on the angular bends at the top, right and left point to the underlying triangular structure. Three circular step patterns in black and white, resembling the decorative studs of glass or enamel on Celtic metalwork, reinforce the importance of the number three.

The decorator of the Book of Durrow used only three colours, as well as the black used to write the text. I have chosen a softer interpretation of the bright, acid colours but not changed their arrangement. The fabric colour suggests the parchment of the manuscript.

The design can be appreciated for the instant impact of the shapes, colour and pattern arrangement, but it also repays closer inspection. The eye traces the path of the bands as they weave their way round the central disc which, by contrast, is an area of stillness and resolution.

Durrow circle Firescreen Firescreen

DESIGN SIZE

37.5 x 49.5cm (14¾ x 19½in) approx.

STITCH COUNT

207 x 272

MATERIALS

50 x 66cm (20 x 26in) biscuit-coloured 28 count Quaker cloth (Zweigart code 323)

⊗

Stranded cotton (floss) as listed

⊗

Tapestry needle size 26

⊗

Firescreen with 41 x 51cm (16 x 20in) aperture approx, or suitable picture frame and brass accessory set with feet and handle (see Suppliers)

1 Prepare your fabric and mark the centre lines with tacking (basting) (see page 107). As this is a more complex design I suggest adding extra guide lines every twenty squares, working outwards from the centre lines. Mount the fabric in an embroidery frame before stitching.

2 Following the chart on pages 60–65 (see diagram below for whole design), cross stitch the embroidery using two strands of stranded cotton (floss) over two threads of the fabric. I suggest working the black straight lines first, then outlining the central disk and its surrounding ring. Work the outlines of the central circle containing the cross and the ones with the black and white (ecru) patterns.

3 Work the interlace patterns and fill in the black background. Now fill in the

DURROW CIRCLE FIRESCREEN
STRANDED COTTONS

COLOUR	DMC	ANCHOR	MADEIRA	SKEINS
Black	310	403	black	6
Gold	3820	306	2209	6
Light gold	676	891	2208	1
Dark gold	782	901	2212	1
Copper red	920	1004	0312	3
Dark copper	918	351	0314	1
Green	470	266	1410	2
Dark green	469	267	1608	1
Ecru	ecru	926	ecrut	5

borders in the gold colours. The broken colour is supposed to suggest the great age of this design. Check for omissions before removing the guide lines.

4 When stitching is complete press the work. Refer to page 108 for advice on stretching your work over a backing card ready to assemble in your firescreen. Then follow the manufacturer's instructions for placing in the firescreen.

The firescreen chart is split over six pages (pages 60–65), with the whole design shown here. For your own use you could colour photocopy the chart parts, enlarge them if you wish, and tape them all together.

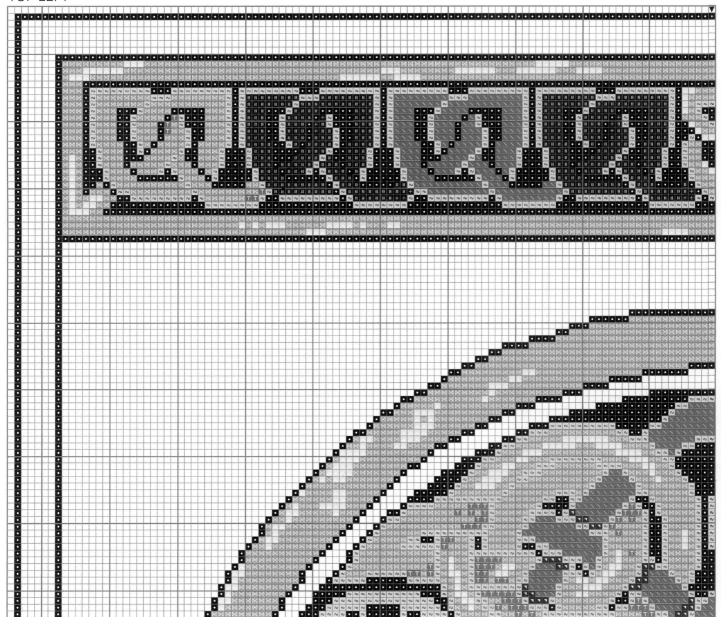

FIRESCREEN
DMC STRANDED COTTONS

◉	310	➕	918
⊠	3820	◥	470
◹	676	◤	469
T	782	∾	ecru
‖	920		

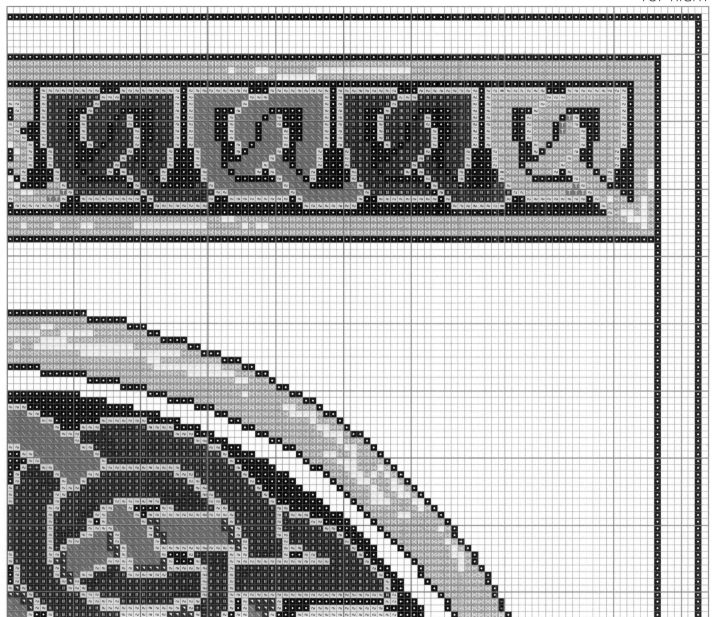

tip

The top band of this design could easily be stitched on its own, to form an impressive towel border or a bookmark. It could also be stitched as a square or rectangle to form a frame around other motifs. As it is closely stitched, it could be used for needlepoint as well as cross stitch, in which case you could use canvas instead of Quaker cloth and tapestry wools (yarns) instead of stranded cottons.

FIRESCREEN
DMC STRANDED COTTONS

●	310	+	918
⊠	3820	◣	470
▢	676	◣	469
T	782	∾	ecru
▊	920		

tip

The central, circular area of the firescreen design could be used to make a fascinating footstool, in either cross stitch with stranded cotton (floss) or in needlepoint with wool (yarn). As this part is so densely stitched it is easy to distort the fabric as you work; it is best therefore, to have the piece well stretched on a frame before you begin stitching.

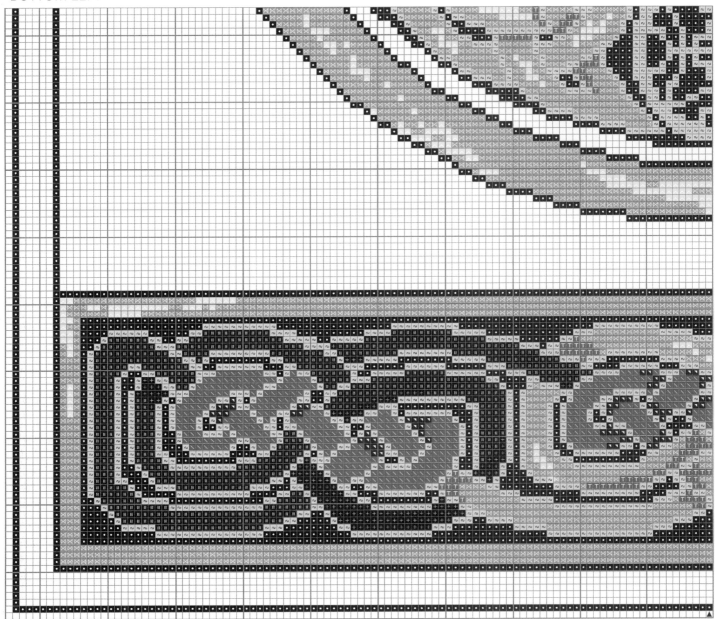

FIRESCREEN
DMC STRANDED COTTONS

⊙	310		✚	918
⊠	3820		◨	470
◺	676		◣	469
T	782		℧	ecru
▥	920			

tip

Th is wonderful broad border at the base of
th firescreen design could be stitched on a
7.5 m (3in) wide Aida band and made up as
a bell-pull. Aida band is particularly good for
bell-pulls because the edges are already nicely
finished and the top and bottom can simply
be folded around the bell-pull ends and
stitched to complete.

Lindisfarne
gospels cushions

The Lindisfarne Gospels, painted around 700 in an Abbey founded in Northumberland by Irish monks, contains such a wealth of inventive designs that I have used it as my inspiration for several projects.

These cushions feature birds and animals, perhaps hawks and hounds. Both designs share a blue interlaced border and a green outer border. The red dotted patterning is a feature of the Lindisfarne Gospel decoration, similar to the punched patterns found on contemporary metal bowls. The bird design was inspired by the opening page of the Gospel of St Matthew. Where the first two large and heavily decorated letters cross, the artist has painted the four entwined birds which dominate the cushion. The diamond pattern which is formed in the embroidery by the blues and yellows of legs and feet, intertwined by the red semicircles which form the central diagonal cross pattern, are copied from the original and form a very satisfying design. It seems to grow in significance as we realize how each element contributes to the geometry of the pattern.

The four hounds design is drawn from the opening page of St John. The first letters are again large and lavishly decorated. The leaping hound and the backward-looking hound form just a minor part of that decoration. I have arranged them to form a square, suitable for a cushion. The red dotted pattern echoes the diagonals and spirals of the hounds.

These cushions feature birds and animals. The birds remind me of ducks around the head, but their feet are eagle-like with powerful talons. The animals have dog-like heads, long jaws, flexible ears and legs and tails which twist and coil.

lindisfarne
birds cushion
gospels cushions

DESIGN SIZE

35.5 x 35.5cm (14 x 14in) approx.

STITCH COUNT

195 x 195

MATERIALS

(for each cushion)

46 x 46cm (18 x 18in) biscuit-
coloured 14 count Aida
(Zweigart code 715)

❧

Stranded cotton (floss) as listed

❧

Tapestry needle size 26

❧

46 x 46cm (18 x 18in) backing
fabric

❧

Cushion pad 40cm (16in) square

❧

2m (2yd) upholstery cord

tip

*Either of these designs could be used to make a
smaller cushion, or a picture, by omitting the
blue border and adding the straight border
around the central design. One of the energetic
hounds would make a lovely picture or a
nameplate for a child's room.*

BIRDS CUSHION
STRANDED COTTONS

COLOUR	DMC	ANCHOR	MADEIRA	SKEINS
Black	310	403	black	4
Pale blue	813	161	1013	4
Mid blue	826	977	1012	1
Light emerald green	913	204	1212	2
Darker green	910	229	1302	1
Coral red	351	10	0214	3
Cream	3823	386	0101	2
Light yellow	3822	305	0109	2
Yellow	3820	306	2209	1

hounds cushion

DESIGN SIZE

35.5 x 35.5cm (14 x 14in) approx.

STITCH COUNT

195 x 195

MATERIALS

As for Birds Cushion

HOUNDS CUSHION
STRANDED COTTONS

COLOUR	DMC	ANCHOR	MADEIRA	SKEINS
Black	310	403	black	5
Pale blue	813	161	1013	4
Light emerald green	913	204	1212	4
Coral red	351	10	0214	2
Darker coral	350	11	0213	1
Cream	3823	386	0101	2
Light yellow	3822	305	0109	2
Yellow	3820	306	2209	1

TO WORK BOTH DESIGNS

1 Prepare your fabric and mark the centre lines with tacking (basting) (see page 107). These are fairly complex designs so I suggest adding extra guide lines at intervals of twenty squares, working outwards from the centre lines.

2 Following the charts on pages 70–73 and 74–77, cross stitch the embroidery using two strands of stranded cotton (floss) over one block of Aida throughout. Be very careful about marking your place and checking the position of one thing against another.

I would begin by working the bands of colour around the animal interlace panels. From there I suggest marking the position of the outer borders before stitching the animal panels.

3 In the hound cushion, the red dotted area is stitched using a shade darker cotton (floss) than is used for the animals. This is because single cross stitches surrounded by fabric tend to appear paler than when stitched as a block of colour.

4 Complete the borders and check for omissions before removing the guide lines. When the embroidery is complete press the work. Refer to page 110 for instructions on making up as a cushion cover. Alternatively, mount and frame as pictures (see page 108).

BIRDS CUSHION
DMC STRANDED COTTONS

●	310	⊓	910
─	813	✚	351
‖	826	⦂	3823
⏄	913	Y	3822
		⋀	3820

BIRDS CUSHION
DMC STRANDED COTTONS

● 310		∿ 910	
— 813		+ 351	
‖ 826		∶ 3823	
⊥ 913		Y 3822	
		∧ 3820	

HOUNDS CUSHION
DMC STRANDED COTTONS

●	310	◥	350
▬	813	:	3823
⊥	913	Y	3822
+	351	◢	3820

HOUNDS CUSHION
DMC STRANDED COTTONS

● 310		◥ 350	
━ 813		⋮ 3823	
⚍ 913		Y 3822	
✚ 351		⌃ 3820	

greedy cat bell-pull

This is another design from an illustration in the inspirational Lindisfarne Gospels and one which would complement the two Lindisfarne Gospels cushions. It is adapted from a border which edges two sides of the Initial page for St Luke's Gospel. In adapting the design to suit a bell-pull shape I removed the right-angled bend, halved the number of birds and extended the tail beyond the bounds of the pink outline to balance the projection of the head. The red diamond pattern, in the original just a band behind the head, I extended to the full length. I felt its regular geometric nature provided a good foil for the complexity of the interwoven birds.

The features that the artist has interlaced are the tails, beaks and claws of the birds and the cat's tail in and out between his legs. Celtic artists were so accustomed to interlacing the extended ears of their creatures that they gave birds a sort of crest as a substitute, and these spiral round the necks, weaving in and out around the tails of the next bird and looping around the claws.

I felt the cat's head was charmingly convincing as a portrait of a cat stalking its prey, whilst at the same time demonstrating the Celtic love of curves and spirals in the shapes of mouth and ears. The same characteristics are seen in the edges of the birds' wings, turned into brightly coloured curves, and the spiral shapes in yellow at the bottom of their heads.

The way the cat's backbone spirals round to line up the back legs with the rest of this bell-pull design marks it out immediately as the work of a Celtic artist, and one with a sense of humour.

greedy cat bell-pull

greedy cat
bell-pull

DESIGN SIZE

12 x 65cm (5 x 25½in) approx.

STITCH COUNT

67 x 358

MATERIALS

25 x 86cm (10 x 34in) biscuit-coloured 14 count Aida (Zweigart code 715)

⅋

Stranded cotton (floss) as listed

⅋

Tapestry needle size 26

⅋

14 x 72cm (5½ x 28½in) pelmet Vilene to interline

⅋

18 x 86cm (7 x 34in) backing fabric

⅋

1.5m (63in) upholstery cord for edging

⅋

14cm (5½in) bell-pull ends (The Viking Loom, model MWP11 No.3 in brass, see Suppliers)

⅋

Tassel (optional)

GREEDY CAT BELL-PULL
STRANDED COTTONS

COLOUR	DMC	ANCHOR	MADEIRA	SKEINS
Black	310	403	black	2
Coral red	351	10	0214	2
Plum pink	3687	68	0604	1
Dark plum	3803	69	0602	1
Very dark plum	902	897	0601	1
Pale blue	813	161	1013	1
Mid blue	826	977	1012	1
Darker blue	825	162	1011	1
Light yellow	3822	305	0109	1
Darker yellow	3852	306	0114	1
Ecru	ecru	926	ecrut	2
Fawn	3782	831	1906	1
Dark grey	844	1041	1810	1

1 Prepare your fabric and mark the centre lines with tacking (basting) (see page 107). Since the embroidery is so long I suggest a further guide line ninety blocks above the centre and another one ninety blocks below.

2 Following the charts, work the cross stitch using two strands of stranded cotton (floss) over one block of Aida. The black backstitch, which is left till last, uses a single strand. Begin near the central guide lines, working enough of the long pink bands to establish a reference point. Continue to stitch, checking your position carefully.

3 When all stitching is finished, check for omissions before removing the guide lines and pressing the work. To make the embroidery up into a bell-pull, follow the instructions on page 109.

**GREEDY CAT
BELL-PULL**

TOP

**DMC STRANDED
COTTONS**

■	310
+	351
≈	3687
◢	3803
⊙	902
−	813
‖	826
⊣	825
Y	3822
▼	3852
▪	ecru
Ɛ	3782
╲	844

Backstitch in
black 310
━━

GREEDY CAT BELL-PULL

MIDDLE

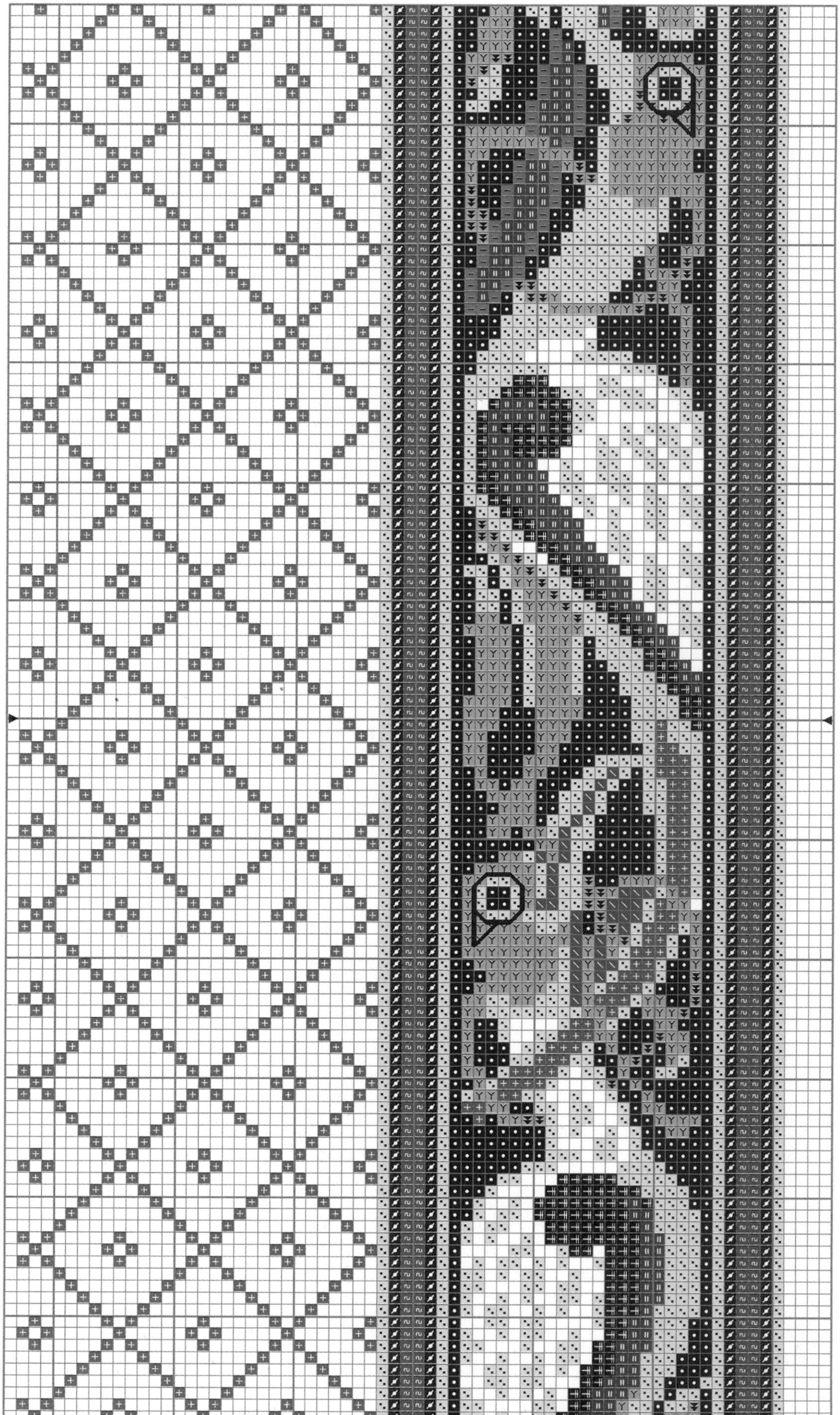

**DMC STRANDED
COTTONS**

■	310
+	351
∼	3687
◢	3803
◉	902
–	813
‖	826
⊣	825
Y	3822
▼	3852
∴	ecru
Ɛ	3782
＼	844

Backstitch in
black 310
━━━

La Tène table linen

The decoration on a helmet worn by a Celt living in Italy in the fourth century BC was the inspiration for this tablecloth. The pattern is typical of the 'La Tène' early Celtic style. The helmet, found in a grave in Canosa di Puglia, was of bronze over iron, decorated with coral studs. Clearly it was intended for display as well as protection. The Celts believed that coral had magical qualities, and could protect the wearer with supernatural power, as well as establish his importance. The bronze relief pattern features fluid spiral shapes, running on into other spirals and into the familiar 'S' scroll or 'lyre' curves. Early examples of this sort of pattern derive from Etruscan designs of palmettes and lotus flowers, but they are transformed in the hands of Celtic artists into never-ending, flowing and merging forms, too abstract to identify but retaining a feeling of organic growth.

The coasters and napkins were based on a bronze bowl from the Ardennes area of France, dating from the same century. I have chosen this triscele pattern with its three radiating spiral 'legs' because the shapes have so much in common with those on the tablecloth. This motif was found right across Celtic Europe. Today it survives in the symbol of the Isle of Man and in Celtic Brittany. It is freestanding on the napkin design but in the coaster the shapes are emphasized by the darker shade which provides a transition to the circular aperture of the coaster.

The tablecloth has been stitched on soft and silky Oslo fabric. The coaster used is a pewter one, chosen partly because its colour sets off the threads and partly because the Celts were such accomplished metalworkers.

84

napkins *la tène table linen*

NAPKINS
STRANDED COTTONS
(for 4)

COLOUR	DMC	ANCHOR	MADEIRA	SKEINS
Blue green	597	168	1110	1
Light blue green	598	167	1111	3
Darker blue green	3810	1066	1109	1
Lightest blue	747	158	1104	1

DESIGN SIZE

10 x 10cm (4 x 4in) approx.

STITCH COUNT

43 x 44

MATERIALS

(for four napkins)

42 x 42cm (16½ x 16½in) antique white 22 count Oslo fabric (Zweigart code 101)

⚭

Stranded cotton (floss) as listed

⚭

Tapestry needle size 26

⚭

Matching sewing thread

tip

Both the tablecloth and napkin designs could be adapted to any evenweave fabric. If you choose a 28 count rather than a 22 count, the overall design size will be smaller. You could also choose different coloured fabrics and threads to suit your china or décor.

1 Prepare the fabric by neatening the edges. Measure in 10cm (4in) from the edges at one corner. Mark the intersection with two pins and centre the guide lines on this point, extending for 5cm (2in) in each direction.

2 Following the chart below, work the design in cross stitch with two strands of stranded cotton (floss) over two double threads of the fabric. Be sure to work in a good light because the colours can be easy to confuse.

3 When all the embroidery is complete remove the tacked (basted) guide lines and press the work carefully. Using an off-white sewing thread, finish around the edges of the napkins with a machined hem, mitring the corners neatly. Alternatively, if you enjoy hand work you could use an antique hem stitch.

NAPKINS
DMC STRANDED COTTONS

597	☐
598	C
3810	◩
747	·

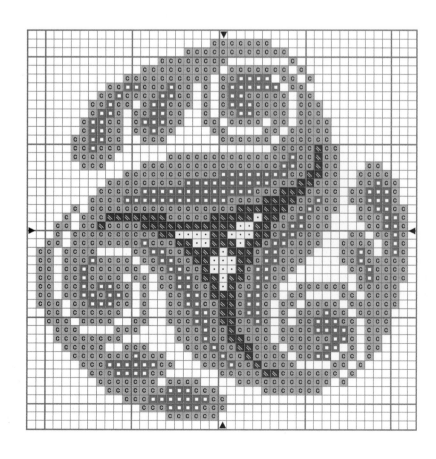

Tablecloth

la tène table linen

COLOUR	DMC	ANCHOR	MADEIRA	SKEINS
Blue green	597	168	1110	7
Light blue green	593	167	1111	2
Darker blue green	3810	1066	1109	2

DESIGN SIZE

42 x 42cm (16½ x 16½in) approx.

STITCH COUNT

180 x 180

MATERIALS

250 x 170cm (98 x 67in) antique white 22 count Oslo fabric (Zweigart code 101)

&

Stranded cotton (floss) as listed

&

Tapestry needle size 26

&

Matching sewing thread

tip

Choose your embroidery cloth to suit the use of the item. For example, the tablecloth has been stitched on Oslo, a cotton fabric like Hardanger but which has a softer, silkier feeling with more drape to it – perfect for a tablecloth.

1 Prepare your fabric and mark the centre lines with tacking (basting) (see page 107). It would also be helpful to mark a grid with tacking (basting) stitches every forty threads (twenty stitches), counting out from the centre lines. Mount the fabric on an embroidery frame to prevent distortion.

2 The design is worked in cross stitch around the centre of the cloth, using two strands of stranded cotton (floss) over two double threads of the fabric. Following the chart on pages 88–91, begin by counting up from the centre to establish a starting point. It may be easiest to work the main colour first.

3 When the embroidery is complete remove the guide lines and carefully press the work. Using an off-white sewing thread, finish round the edges with a machined hem, mitring the corners neatly (see page 108).

TABLECLOTH
DMC STRANDED COTTONS

☐ 597

C 598

▨ 3810

TABLECLOTH
DMC STRANDED COTTONS

	597
C	598
/	3810

COASTERS

la tène table linen

COASTERS
STRANDED COTTONS
(for 4)

COLOUR	DMC	ANCHOR	MADEIRA	SKEINS
Lightest blue	747	158	1104	2
Light blue green	598	167	1111	1
Darker blue green	3810	168	1109	1
Very dark blue green	3808	170	1108	1

DESIGN SIZE

7.5 x 7.5cm (3 x 3in) approx.

STITCH COUNT

41 x 41

MATERIALS (for four coasters)

Four 15cm (6in) squares of white or pale-coloured 14 count Aida

❀

Stranded cotton (floss) as listed

❀

Tapestry needle size 26

❀

Firm iron-on interfacing

❀

Four pewter coasters
(The Viking Loom, see Suppliers)

COASTERS
DMC STRANDED COTTONS

·	747
C	598
◩	3810
↑	3808

1 Prepare the fabric and mark the centre lines with tacking (basting) (see page 107). Following the chart, stitch the design in cross stitch using two strands of stranded cotton (floss) over one block of Aida. Work in a good light because the colours are easy to confuse.

2 When the embroidery is complete, remove the guide lines and press the work. Iron the interfacing on to the back of the embroidery, according to the manufacturer's instructions.

3 Mark the circular edge of the embroidery using the glass or template from the coaster as a guide and then cut out neatly. Now assemble the embroidery in the coaster according to the manufacturer's instructions. If using a plastic coaster, which is a little larger than the one shown, there will be a narrow margin of the fabric showing round the edges. This could be filled in with cross stitches using the darkest colour thread.

Celtic motif library

The following pages contain more than fifty small designs from which you can choose individual motifs or combine several in your own projects. The colours used in this section are just suggestions so no keys have been included but there is information about the designs and what you might do with them.

1–6 FROM FOURTH CENTURY BC – SEVENTH CENTURY AD

1 This design is taken from a shoulder clasp from the early seventh century and discovered during the excavation of the burial of an Anglo Saxon ruler at Sutton Hoo, Suffolk, England. The shoulder clasps are of gold inlaid with garnets and millefiori glass (giving the chequered effect). Try using it for a card, a notebook cover or a pincushion. I would choose a fabric in one of the blues or reds. It would also lend itself to being worked in needlepoint. It is an easy design to increase or reduce in size.

2 This serpent forms one of the borders of the shoulder clasp above, as is No.45. I suggest working it on a bookmark using a bright yellow background to echo the gold of the original.

3 This comes from a gold buckle which was part of the Sutton Hoo hoard. Again, it would be ideal for a bookmark, perhaps with a ribbon or tassel knotted through the end of the tail.

4 A serpentine decoration from a spearhead from Hungary, dating from the fourth and third centuries BC. I am astonished by the similarity of the creatures to the ones from Sutton Hoo 1,000 years later. This would be effective displayed in a card with an oval aperture or in an oval flexi-hoop as a picture.

5 This comes from a carved stone pillar from Germany, the same date as No.4. I find this a very satisfying image, suggesting ripe seed-heads but also animals' heads, with eyes and open jaws. It could be repeated to form a border for towels or tie-backs or be used for a small card or to fill in part of a larger design.

6 This comes from a fourth century BC gold bracelet, from Waldalgesheim, Germany. It is just one of a wide range of patterns formed when triscele motifs are combined.

7–10 FOLIAGE FROM MANUSCRIPT PAINTINGS

7 A tree of life motif from the Litchfield Gospels. You could record the names of parents and children on either side of the trunk, or perhaps combine it with the deer (No.31).

8 A border from the Book of Kells. Just the very top and bottom have been embroidered in the worked example, left.

This could be used as a card or bookmark or perhaps a spectacles case. It can be worked longer or shorter. Try adding bands of the colours used at top and bottom to finish off.

9 Part of another border from the same page of the Book of Kells. Like No.8 it was a horizontal not a vertical border. Try copying it and turning it through 180 degrees then combine the two to form a symmetrical border for the top or bottom of a sampler or the edge of a table-mat.

10 From a different page of the Book of Kells, this foliage flourish filled one side of a semicircular arch. Notice how the leaves are made of three parts, a magical Celtic number. Consider using this in the corner of a mat or napkin, or using it with a mirror-image copy at the top of a design of your making.

11–14 LA TÈNE (EARLY CELTIC) BORDERS

11 This is a favourite of mine dating from third century BC Ireland. It would make an excellent border for table linen or perhaps to apply a decorative touch to the bottom edge of a plain roller blind.

12 A pattern from a bronze helmet from France, fifth/fourth century BC. The chart shows a continuous border, but if you stop at the diagonal motifs it makes an effective finish for the top and bottom of a sampler.

13 This is based on a pattern from a bracelet, from France in the third century BC. Use it as part of a picture or on the edge of a guest towel.

14 A continuous pattern made from triscele motifs. This was painted on a pot in Champagne, France in the fourth century BC. The chart shows two repeats with modified versions at either end. Repeat the inner motifs for a longer border.

15–21 BORDERS, MOSTLY FROM MANUSCRIPT PAINTINGS

15 This is one of the most frequently used borders in the Gospel books. I have included corners for all these designs so a complete frame can be worked, although they can also be used for straight borders.

16 This is quite a complex border. It can be continuous or you can close the ends.

17 A simple but striking border where it is easy to see the repeats. Good for simple bookmarks, or choose one motif on its own where a small pattern is needed.

18 This fretwork pattern is from a carving on a Celtic cross. If you add extra repeats, keep the zigzag pattern consistent.

19 A complex braid from the Book of Durrow. I have added a fourth colour to the original three to make it clearer.

20 This is based on the twisted strands of gold in Celtic torcs. I have shown corners with the lighter and darker colours bending over so that it will make almost any size. It would combine well with other wider borders.

21 Another border from the Book of Durrow with simple repeats.

22–27 MAINLY HORSES, WITH A FIERCE, PRIMITIVE ENERGY

22 Horses were sacred to the Celts, symbolized by the goddess Epona. This design, from a first century BC coin found in Bratislava, is particularly suitable for mounting in a circular frame, perhaps for a pot lid or small picture.

23 Bursting with energy, this hound-like creature comes from a silver hoard found in St Ninian's Isle, Shetland and dates from the eighth century. Use it by itself or choose a border to surround it.

24 A cat from the Book of Kells, which could make a coaster or perhaps a simple card.

25 From a first century BC coin found in Bratislava, this design had the space under the horse's body occupied by words. If making this into a circular picture, a name or greeting could be added.

26 A horse and rider from a procession on the first century BC Gundestrup Cauldron, from Denmark. The helmet is topped by a sculpted hawk.

27 From another first century BC coin found in Bratislava. I am sure this is a horse but it seems to have several characteristics of a lion, perhaps to give it extra ferocity. Again, it would fit on a round or square coaster or card.

28–32 VARIOUS CREATURES

28 A fish motif from the Book of Kells. It could be used in a sampler with other motifs, or try working three in a column for a card for a fishing fanatic. Try different colours for each fish.

29 A bird from the Book of Kells. The picture, left, shows this in an oval flexi-hoop but it might be fun worked on a child's pocket, either using waste canvas or applying an Aida patch.

30 A fine, dignified stag from a carved stone slab from Ireland, about 800 AD.

31 Another deer from a stone carving. The spots are not original. This is suitable for a square frame or could be incorporated into a larger sampler.

32 This a from a Pictish carved cross slab from Dunfallandy in Scotland. It could be elaborated with a colour fill of the body and perhaps the addition of a frame made from one of the border patterns.

33–37 A SELECTION OF CONTINUOUS STRAND PATTERNS

33 I like the way this links square and triangular ideas. Worked on 16 or 18 count Aida it would make an attractive square coaster or look good if worked on a small bag or pincushion.

34 I took this idea from a manuscript painting. It would make a good card or could be stitched in the corners of table linen.

35 This came from the Book of Kells, but similar motifs abound. It would fit well into a card with a circular aperture.

36 From a carving on a cross, this can also be used horizontally.

37 A wonderful combination of triangle and circle from the Lindisfarne Gospels.

38–43 SQUARES AND CROSSES

38 One of the step patterns from the Lindisfarne Gospels, part of one of the Carpet pages. To fill a square coaster it would need a coloured border, suggested on the chart.

39 This design and No.41 are simplified versions of a stone carving decorating an archway. This one shows the design in a variety of related shades. Variegated thread might produce a similar effect.

40 A simple but striking design copied from a Welsh cross. It would be suitable for any small project or the corner of a larger one.

41 This version uses just three colours and was worked on 7.5cm (3in) wide Aida band to make the bag shown above.

42 Another version of the design from the Lindisfarne Gospels. See No.38.

43 This decoration is from the side of a metal, house-shaped casket and was one of three, each surrounded by a circle, making it ideal for a circular coaster or card.

44–48 POT-POURRI

44 From another page of the Lindisfarne Gospels. This also would look good as a coaster, with or without the blue border, or would make a nice pincushion or needlecase.

45 Another Sutton Hoo border, most suitable for a bookmark.

46 This design from a Carpet page in the Book of Durrow is very suitable for a pincushion.

47 This is one of the designs associated with the Celtic culture of Brittany, and clearly derives from the triscele motif.

48 Another design from Brittany. I suggest adding them to a larger design, or perhaps repeating and arranging them to form your own design.

49–53 MORE SERPENTS

49 From the Sutton Hoo belt buckle, this design has been coloured to make the two serpents easier to trace. I see it as a picture in a circular aperture mount, or maybe worked as a pincushion.

50 This design (shown right) is from the Book of Kells, repeated five times at the base of a colonnace. Each design is enclosed by a circular border within a wider circular border. This makes it very suitable for anything round. It is worked as a card in the picture, but would have been equally suitable for a coaster or pot lid.

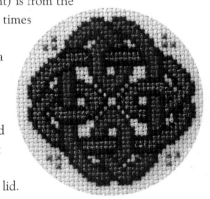

51 Another design from a manuscript painting, again using a continuous strand. It would look effective worked in gold thread for a special card.

52 Inspired by the serpents of the Book of Kells, this would make a good notebook cover or perhaps the lid of a little box.

53 This is another of the creatures which decorates the text areas of the Book of Kells. This one wriggles between two lines of text, so might combine well with a child's name.

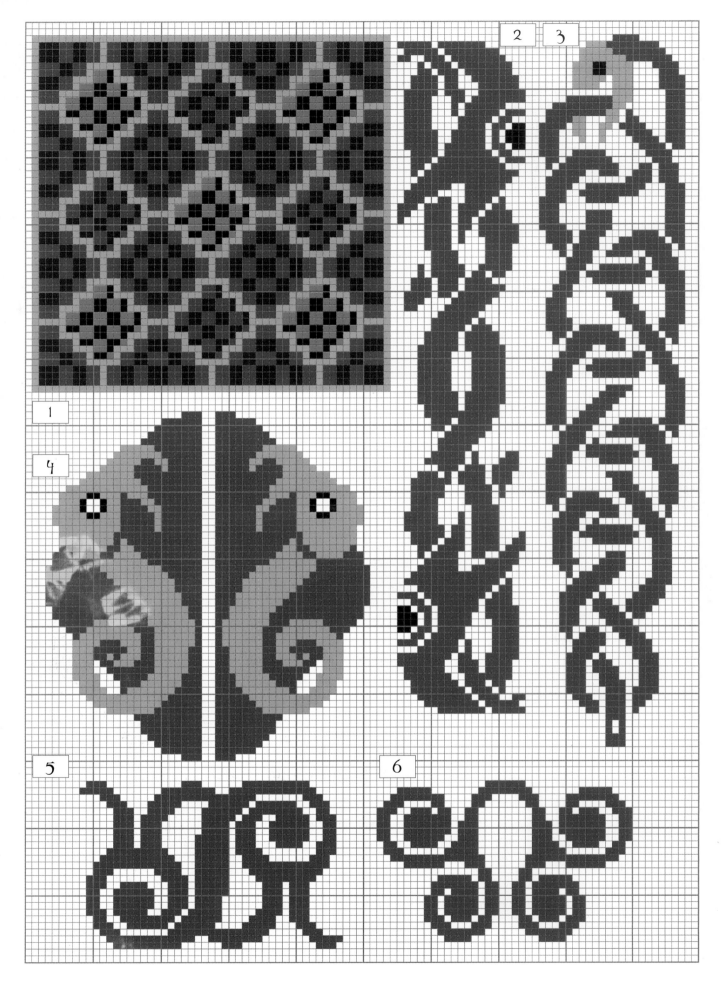

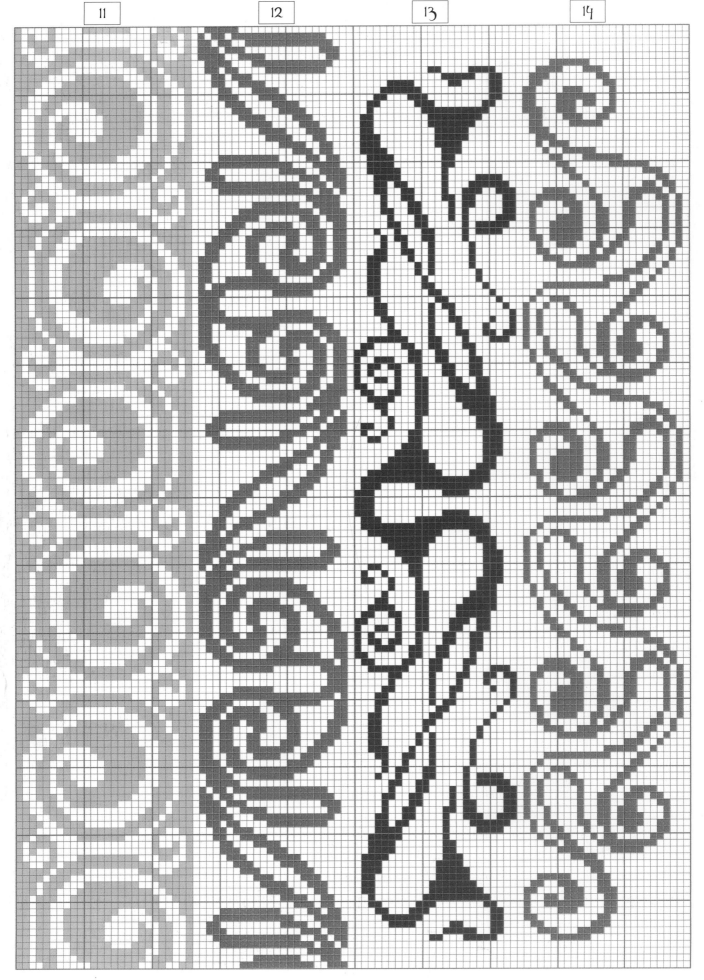

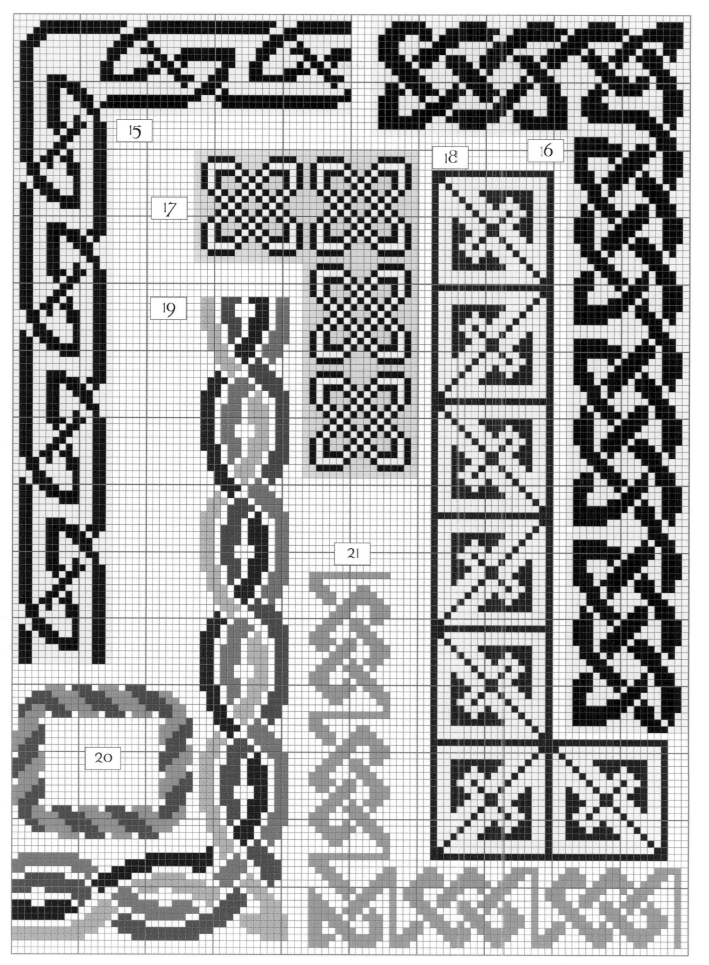

28

29

30

31

32

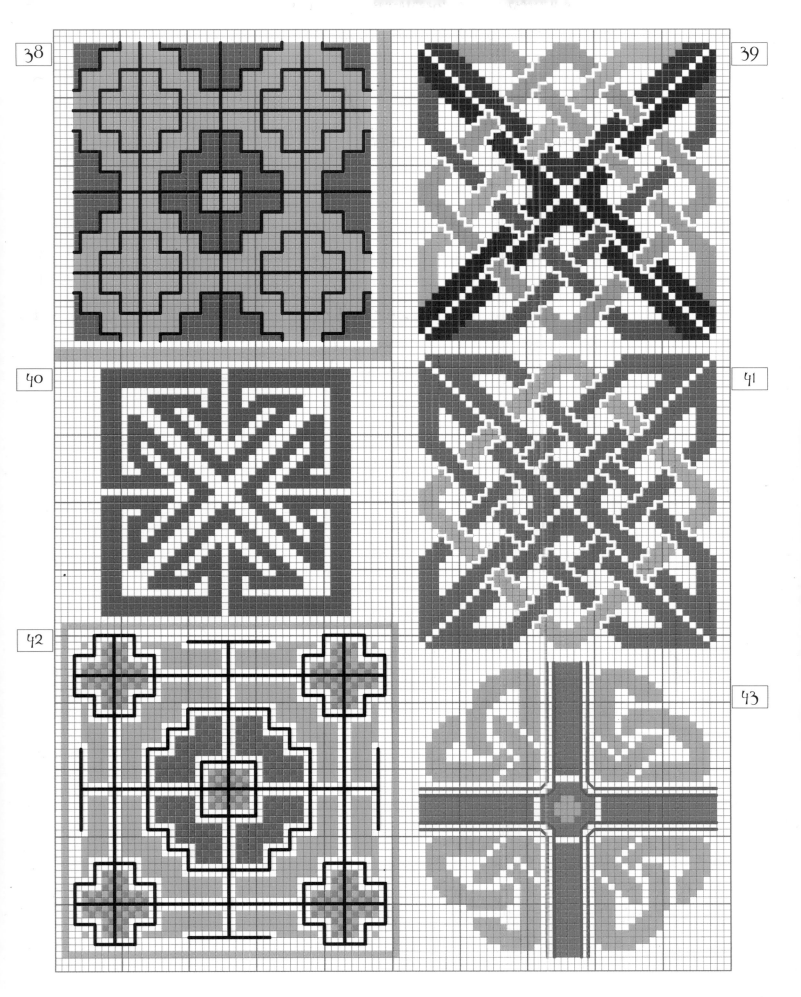

MATERIALS, TECHNIQUES AND MAKING UP

MATERIALS

Those who have not done much embroidery before will find the following pages both useful and informative.

Fabrics

The projects in this book list exactly the fabric required for working the piece as in the photograph but you could substitute one fabric for another.

Aida is a blockweave fabric which is probably the simplest to work. The weave locks each block of threads in place resulting in a very stable, firm fabric. Stitching is usually over one block.

Evenweave fabric, such as linen, is one which has the same number of warp threads as weft threads to 1in or 2.5cm. An evenweave is usually embroidered over two threads at a time, thus a 28 h.p.i. (holes per inch) evenweave fabric can be substituted for a 14 h.p.i. Aida, a 32 h.p.i. evenweave for a 16 h.p.i. Aida – and vice versa.

Calculating Design Size

You may want to work on a larger or smaller grade of fabric to create a finished piece of a slightly different size. To determine design size, divide the stitch count by the number of holes per inch of the fabric.

Remember also that most designs need a margin of blank fabric round the edge of the stitched area, plus more for making up. The amounts of fabric listed in the projects allow for this. If you work it out for yourself allow at least 5cm (2in) extra on all sides. Where measurements are given the width is quoted first, followed by height.

Threads

Stranded cotton (floss) is used in many of the projects. I've used DMC but if you prefer one of the alternatives given bear in mind that they are not always an exact colour match. The names I have used are for convenience and are not official ones. Always order by the number. Divide skeins into lengths of about 50cm (20in) and divide each length into its six strands. Recombine the number needed – usually two.

Rayon floss can be divided in the same way as stranded cotton into separate strands. It gives a lovely sheen but can take a little getting used to. For best results use a good, non-greasy hand cream so that your skin does not catch the thread. Cut shorter lengths than usual – about 30cm (12in). Select the required number of threads, then, especially if you are working in a dry atmosphere, draw the strands over a damp sponge which helps them to lie flat. Finish off neatly by threading the

end of the thread through the back of several stitches and cutting it neatly so it cannot fluff out.

Metallic embroidery floss gives an extra sparkle to a design and can also be divided into the required number of strands. DMC recommend using lengths of only 30cm (12in). Select a new length if the thread shows any signs of damage.

Metallic braid is used as it comes. I have used a Kreinik metallic braid in the Tara Dragons Picture and Dragons Box.

Needles

All the embroidery is done with blunt-ended tapestry needles. I have recommended sizes but you may prefer a size larger or smaller. It is a compromise between having a large enough eye to take the thread but which will pass through the fabric holes without too much friction.

General Accessories

Apart from fabric, thread and needles you must have a good pair of embroidery scissors with sharp points, as well as cutting out scissors. I think a bright light is essential, preferably with a 'daylight' bulb. When you work on dark fabrics it is helpful to place a brightly reflective sheet of paper or white pillow slip over your knees to make the holes in the fabric show up more clearly. Working some designs is much easier with a magnifier.

Frames

I recommend using a frame for any evenweave fabric and when working with a mixture of threads as you may pull some threads more firmly than others. Small pieces of Aida can be worked without a frame. For small pieces, a hoop frame or flexi-hoop will be suitable. Always try to use a frame large enough to take the whole of the design. If this is not possible then only leave the frame on the work whilst you are actually embroidering, and take care when repositioning it not to let the edge coincide with an embroidered area.

For larger pieces a rectangular 'slate' frame is the traditional answer. The embroidery fabric is stitched to a tape attached to the top and bottom rails. Some versions have other ways of securing the fabric. The rails can be rotated to store fabric rolled round them if the fabric is larger than the frame. The edges of the selected area are laced to the sides of the frame to keep the fabric taut.

Another type of frame is the rectangular clip frame, made from lengths of plastic tube. The fabric is placed over the tubes and clipped in place, using extra tubes, slit along their length. This frame is particularly suitable where part of a large volume of fabric is being worked.

Techniques

This section is well worth reading as it describes how to prepare for work and how to work the stitches.

Preparing the Fabric

If working on Aida, cutting with pinking shears is sufficient to stop it from fraying. If using evenweave, neaten the edges with a machine zigzag stitch or by overcasting the edges by hand.

Centre lines are indicated on the charts by opposing arrows. Find the centre of your fabric by folding it in half both ways. Mark the centre lines in sewing thread, using tacking (basting), making sure that the line of stitches stays straight along the grain of the fabric. In some of the larger designs I have suggested marking extra guide lines because they are quite complex. It is wise to choose one colour for the centre lines and another for any other lines.

Following the Charts

Each coloured square on the charts represents one cross stitch. The chart keys list the threads used and their codes, while the thread lists within the projects include alternatives to DMC stranded cotton (floss) where appropriate. Symbols have been added for greater ease of identification in all the charts except in the Celtic Motif Library and Celtic Key desk set. Where backstitch is used it is represented as a thick, coloured line.

The charts have more pronounced lines every ten squares to help you to count. You can photocopy the charts for your own use, enlarging them and taping together sections of the larger charts. You can then cross off areas as you work them, which some people find helpful. It also allows you to draw in the centre lines and any extra guide lines in felt pen to match the guide lines you have worked. As a general rule I start embroidering at the centre and work blocks of colour at a time.

Starting and Finishing

To begin stitching, knot the thread then take it through the fabric from the front about 2.5cm (1in) from the beginning point. When you have stitched over the thread the knot can be trimmed off and the end persuaded through to the back. To start a new thread in a stitched area just thread it under four or five stitches on the back before beginning to stitch.

To finish off, thread your needle back through the last four or five stitches on the wrong side of the fabric. With stranded cotton (floss) this is all that is needed. Simply trim the thread.

When working with rayon floss I thread the needle through two or three stitches, then take it back one and repeat.

Washing and Ironing

The current advice when washing embroidery is to wash in water, as hot as the fabric will stand. Use a mild detergent, thoroughly dissolved. If the colour does bleed then separate the item, wash it thoroughly without rubbing, and rinse until all trace of the stain disappears. Never leave it wet. Remove excess water by rolling the item in a towel and squeezing gently. Dry it flat, then iron from the back whilst still damp.

Careful pressing will smooth out the fabric and correct any distortion without flattening the stitches and spoiling the texture. A layer of towel covered with a piece of sheet should give a soft enough surface. Lay the embroidery face down on the surface and pull it into shape, making sure that the grain of the fabric is straight. Press it gently on the back at a heat suitable for the type of fabric and thread. Do not use steam on metallic threads and cover the piece with a pressing cloth.

Cottons embroidered on Aida or cotton cloth can be pressed at the two- to three-spot setting; anything involving synthetic fabric or thread requires a cooler, one-spot setting.

Stitches

There are very few stitches required to complete the projects in this book. Whole cross stitch is the basic stitch used, with no fractional stitches.

Cross Stitch

Either work individual cross stitches, or half crosses along a line, then return, stitching over the half crosses in the opposite direction. The first method is the most stable and unlikely to cause distortion. So long as you develop an even tension, without pulling the stitch so tightly that it distorts the fabric, either is suitable. Choose which direction your top stitch will go and stick to it. It is important to do this otherwise the texture will be uneven. Figs 1 and 2 show cross stitch worked over one block of Aida and two threads of evenweave.

Fig 1

Fig 2

Backstitch

This is an easy outline stitch that gives extra definition or detail to a design. It is used in the Book of Kells Peacock Picture on page 30 and in the Greedy Cat Bell-pull on page 80. The project instructions say whether the backstitch should be worked with one or two strands of stranded cotton (floss). It is usually worked after all the cross stitch has been completed. This also helps to stop the backstitch becoming 'lost' beneath the rest of the stitching.

To work backstitch, bring the needle through the fabric from the back. Take a stitch backwards. Bring the needle up again at the far end of the next stitch along the line. Take another stitch backwards to fill in the gap (Fig 3). Work over the same unit of fabric – one block or two threads – as you have used for the cross stitch.

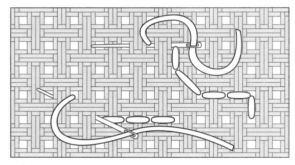

Fig 3

Ladder Stitch

This is a neat way of joining the edges of two pieces of fabric which have already been neatened, or have turnings. It is used in the Spectacles Case on page 26 to join the embroidered case to its lining fabric, and also when making up a book cover, as described on page 109.

To work ladder stitch, bring the needle out through the edge at one side, then take it straight across into the other edge. Slip the needle through the edge a little way and take a stitch back to the first side, making another rung on the ladder. Repeat as shown in Fig 4.

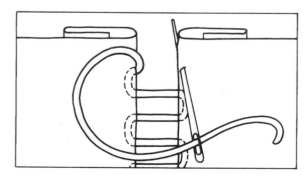

Fig 4

MAKING UP

This section describes how to make up the projects as they are shown throughout the book.

Pictures

To make your work up into a picture you can simply press it and take it to a framer specializing in embroidery to do the rest. If you prefer to do it yourself, read on. The embroidery will need attaching to a piece of mount board (stiff card) which fits inside the frame. Use white board for pale-coloured fabrics and dark card for darker fabrics. When framing behind a mount I sometimes just glue the embroidery to the card around the extreme edges. (Never allow glue on an area where it could be seen as a stain can develop over time.) I have also used double-sided tape or occasionally staples.

If the piece is to be framed without a mount then it should be laced round the card. This also cures any wrinkles or distortions. Cut the card to fit easily inside the frame, remembering to allow for the thickness of fabric pulled round the edge. Mark the centre of each side on the back of the card and where you want the centre of the embroidery to be. Lay the front of the card on the wrong side of the fabric, matching

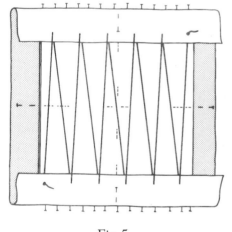

Fig 5

the centre marks. Fold the fabric round the board and hold in place by pushing pins through into the edge of the card. Start at the centres and work outwards on opposite sides. Check that the fabric is held taut and that the grain is straight. When you are satisfied, take a long length of buttonhole or linen thread and lace from side to side, pulling the thread tightly enough to hold the fabric firmly in place without bending the card (Fig 5). Repeat with the other two sides. I prefer to frame without glass, but if you choose glass ask the framer not to squash it up against the embroidery, flattening its texture.

Mitring Corners

This is a neat method of removing excess fabric from a corner and is a good way to finish napkins and similar items. Fold the fabric in the required amount and mark the fold line, then unfold the turnings. At the corner fold the fabric on the diagonal as in Fig 6 and press the crease. Allowing for a small turning along the creased side, trim away the excess fabric. Turn in the long edges and the creased diagonal sides should meet in a neat mitre. Stitch them together invisibly.

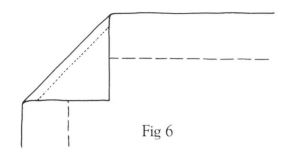

Fig 6

Using Fusible Interfacing

Fusible (iron-on) interfacing is useful for small projects where the fabric needs to be trimmed to fit a lid or paperweight and there is no room for turnings. It is available in white and black for light or dark projects. Once ironed on it stabilizes the fabric threads, allowing the exact shape to be cut out without fear of fraying. Always press the embroidery before adding the interfacing. Try a small sample on the fabric you are using first.

Bell-pull

Bell-pulls are a good way of displaying embroidery. The Greedy Cat embroidery is made up into a bell-pull as follows. Begin by folding in the long edges four blocks out from the edge of the red border which forms the top and bottom of the design. Trim off some of the excess fabric leaving a seam allowance of about 2.5cm (1in). If using a cord with a tape edging, position this next, tacking (basting) it in place before stitching to the embroidered fabric along the fold.

Check the exact width of your embroidery and cut the interfacing marginally narrower. Place it in position to back the area which will be visible. Fold the seam allowance over it and secure in position with some stitches which do not pierce right through to the embroidery. Fold over the long edges of the backing fabric so that it fits neatly on the back of the bell-pull. Tack (baste) in place and stitch to the bell-pull by hand.

Now attach the bell-pull ends. Those I used have a bar at the back which clamps to the visible part at the front, hiding the top and bottom edges. Position the ends six blocks out from the red bands, passing the metal connecting rods through between the cord edging and embroidered fabric. Mark the finished length and then trim the fabric sandwich marginally shorter so that the raw edges will not be visible at the top and bottom. If you have bell-pull ends with a bar, – fold the fabric round the bar. Decide how long the fold back needs to be before trimming and neatening the ends of the fabric. Attach a tassel as a finishing touch if you wish.

Book Cover

Many of the designs could be used to cover books. These instructions apply to the Celtic Key notebook cover on page 36 but the method can be used to make all sorts of covers.

Begin by measuring from the opening edge of your book, round the spine to the other edge. Cut the fusible interfacing this length x the height of the book and bond it to the back of the fabric so that it interlines the two covers and spine.

Turn in all the edges producing a long strip which you can wrap round the front cover, the spine and the back cover (see Fig 7). On the insides of the covers the fabric should come to within about 1.25cm (½in) of the extreme left and right. Press all folds.

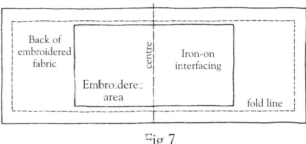

Fig 7

Wrap around the book to check the fit and then ladder stitch along at top and bottom to form two pockets for the front and back covers (Fig 8). Slip the book covers into the pockets. It should be a close fit, but not so tight that the book will not close completely.

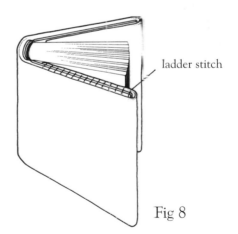

ladder stitch

Fig 8

Box Lid

To mount embroidery in a box top, as in the Needlework Box on page 12 and Dragons Box on page 47, leave the guide lines in to help position the embroidery over the pad. Stretch over the pad and tack down according to the manufacturer's instructions, or stretch over the pad as over card for a picture, using linen thread (see page 108). Remove the guide lines.

A piping cord with a tape edging can then be tacked (basted) to the edge of the pad as an outline for the design or to conceal any gap. Before assembling in the lid, cover the bottom of the pad with a piece of fabric or card, stuck or stapled round the edge.

Cushion

Many of the designs in the book would make wonderful cushions. To make up the Lindisfarne Cushions on page 66, begin by marking exactly where you want the edge to be, bearing in mind your cushion pad size. Choose a backing fabric which matches the embroidered fabric or tones with it and cut this to the finished size, plus turnings. Place the fabrics right sides together and pin them. Machine stitch with the wrong side of the embroidered fabric uppermost, following the edge line you marked. Start a little way from one corner, go around three sides and finish by stitching a little way round the last corner, leaving a gap to put the cushion pad through. Work another line of stitching round the corners to reinforce. Cut diagonally across the corners quite close to the stitching, and trim the other edges, leaving the usual seam allowance. Turn the cushion to the right side and press the seam. Insert the pad and stitch the edges together. Optionally, you could add decorative cord or piping round the edges.

An alternative method is to make up the backing piece with a zip inserted. To do this you need a slightly larger backing piece, cut in half. Place the two halves right sides together. Sew 5cm (2in) of the seam at the top and bottom and insert a zip in the gap. Proceed as above but sew round all four sides. Open the zip to turn the cushion and insert the pad.

Needlecase

The needlecase on page 16 has a finished size of 9.5 x 12.5cm (3¾ x 5in) and is made up in the following way. Begin by ironing the interfacing on the back of the embroidered fabric. Allowing a seam allowance all round the interfaced area, trim away excess fabric. Pin the embroidery and the backing fabric together with right sides facing and stitch around three and a half sides, leaving a gap at the back. Turn right side out and then ladder stitch the gap together. This piece will be folded to produce the front and back of the needlecase.

Trim the felt for the inner 'pages', perhaps with pinking shears. Place it in the centre of the backing fabric (to make two pages) and pin in place. Turn the embroidery over and prepare to stitch the pages together along the fold. Measure out 4cm (1½in) either side of the centre and mark with a pin.

Ignoring the centre mark, divide the space between into three equal parts. Using a large needle and a cord made from leftover cottons (floss) (use all six strands), make a stitch through from the outside at the second mark down, going through both thicknesses. Leave a length on the outside. Bring the needle back to the outside at the top mark. Take the cord back through at or near the second mark, out to the outside again at the third mark, in again at the fourth and back again at or near the third. Knot the ends, then make a bow or tassel, fringe out the ends and trim. Press from the back to finish.

Pincushion and Scissor Keeper

To make up a pincushion or scissor keeper, as on pages 14 and 17, take your embroidered piece and trim away excess fabric. Cut out backing fabric to the same size. If using a braid with a tape edging, position it with the braid on the inside of the stitching line and the tape towards the edge, then tack (baste) in place. Pin the embroidery and the backing together with right sides facing. With matching sewing thread, stitch round three sides, continuing a little way round both corners into the fourth side. Turn right side out and fill with polyester stuffing, then stitch up the gap to complete.

Alternatively, a scissor keeper can be finished off with a twisted braid made from leftover cotton (floss) or a bought fine braid and a tassel. Fold the braid in half and make a knot about 18cm (7in) from the fold. Attach the braid to one corner at the knot. Slipstitch the braid all around the edges, knotting again at the opposite corner. Fringe out the ends to make a tassel, then trim neatly. Thread the loop through one of the handles of the scissors, then pass the scissors though the loop.

Acknowledgments

Acknowledgments go to companies who have been very helpful and generous in providing materials and accessories. My thanks to DMC for fabrics and threads and especially to Cara for her help and advice, to Kreinik for metallic threads, to Fabric Flair for fabrics, to Framecraft for accessories including the decorative bowl, handbag mirror, key ring and paperweight, and The Viking Loom who supplied bell-pull ends and coasters.

My thanks to my editor Cheryl Brown for her continued help, support and encouragement. To Lin Clements, the project editor, for her hard work in shaping and co-ordinating. To the art editor Ali Myer and to Lisa Forrester for the book design. Thanks to Ethan Danielson for his work on the charts, and to the photographer Stewart Grant, who has made all the designs look so wonderful. Lastly, to all my family for all their help and support.

Suppliers

For Zweigart fabrics and DMC threads
DMC Creative World Ltd
Pullman Road, Wigston,
Leicestershire LE18 2DY, UK
tel: 0116 2811040
fax: 0116 2813592
website: www.dmc.com

Willow Fabrics (mail order)
95 Town Lane, Mobberley,
Cheshire WA16 7HH, UK
tel: 0800 0567811
website: www.willowfabrics.com

Joan Toggitt Ltd,
2 Riverview Drive, Somerset,
NJ 08873, USA
tel: 908 2711949
fax: 908 2710758

For Fabric Flair embroidery fabrics
Fabric Flair Ltd
The Old Brewery, The Close,
Warminster, Wilts BA12 9AL, UK
tel: 0800 716 851
fax: 01985 846849
website: www.fabricflair.com

*For Anchor stranded cotton (floss) and
Kreinik metallic threads*
Coats Craft UK
PO Box 22, Lingfield House,
Lingfield Point, McMullen Rd, Darlington,
County Durham DL1 1YQ, UK
tel: 01325 394237
website: www.coatscrafts.co.uk

Coats and Clark,
4135 South Stream Boulevard,
Charlotte, North Carolina 28217, USA
tel: 704 329 5016
fax: 704 329 5027

For Kreinik metallic threads
Kreinik Manufacturing Co Inc
3106 Titmanus Lane, Suite#101,
Baltimore, MD 21244, USA
tel: 1 800 537 2166
website: www.kreinik.com

For Madeira embroidery threads
Barnyarns Ltd, (mail order)
PO Box 28, Thirsk, North Yorkshire
YO7 3YN, UK
tel: 01423 326423
fax 01423 326221
website: www.barnyarns.com

Madeira (USA) Ltd,
PO Box 6068, 30 Bayside Court,
Laconia, NH03246, USA
tel: 603 5282944
fax: 603 528 4264

For cards
Craft Creations Ltd
Ingersoll House, Delamere Rd, Cheshunt,
Hertfordshire EN8 9HD, UK
tel: 01992 781900
website: www.craftcreations.com

*For trinket pots, paperweight, handbag mirror
and key ring*
Framecraft Miniatures Ltd
372–376 Summer Lane, Hockley,
Birmingham B19 3QA, UK
tel: 0121 212 0551
fax 0121 212 0552
website: www.framecraft.com

Anne Brinkley Designs
761 Palmer Avenue, Holmdel
NJ 07733, USA
tel: 908 787 2011

Gar Bowles Sales Inc
PC Box 1060, Janesville,
WB 53547, USA
tel: 508 754 9212
fax 608 754 0665

For bell-puil ends and coasters
The Viking Loom
22 High Petergate, York, YO1 7EH, UK
tel/fax: 01904 765599
website: www.vikingloom.co.uk

For workboxes, trinket boxes and firescreens
Market Square (Warminster) Ltd
Wine Farm, Longbridge Deverill,
Warminster, Wiltshire BA12 7DD, UK
tel: 01985 841041
fax: 01985 541042

For circular wooden picture frames
Turnstyle Crafted Wooden Products
2 Slave Hill, Haddenham, Bucks,
HP17 8AY, UK
tel/fax: 01844 290520

*For brass firescreen accessories
(feet and handle to fit on a picture frame)*
**Peter Hodson Quality Picture Frames
and Gallery**
44–48 Coronation Road, Cleethorpes,
North East Lincolnshire DN35 8RS, UK
tel/fax: 01472 604853

Barbara Hammet designs
Including Celtic cross designs in blackwork
and canvaswork
tel: 01462 853862
website www.wessexcollection.co.uk

Bibliography

Backhouse J. *The Lindisfarne Gospels* (Phaidon, 1981)
Green M. *Celtic Art Reading the Messages* (Everyman Art Library, 1996)
Kruta V. (ed), Frey O. H., Saftery B. & Tsabo M. *The Celts*
    (Thames & Hudson, 1991)
Laing L. & Laing J. *Art of the Celts* (Thames & Hudson, 1992, 1994)
Meehan B. *The Book of Durrow* (Town Ho, Dublin, 1996)
Meehan B. *The Book of Kells* (Thames & Hudson, 1994, 2000)
Nordenfalk C. *Celtic and Anglo-Saxon Painting* (Chatto & Windus, 1977)
Romilly Allen J. *Celtic Art* (Senate, imprint of Tiger Books International plc,
    reprinted 1997 from first publication 1904)
Seaborne M. *Celtic Crosses of Britain and Ireland* (Shire Archeology, 1994)
Stead I. *Celtic Art* (British Museum, 1985, 1996)
Stead I. & Hughes K. *Early Celtic Designs, British Museum Pattern Books*
    (British Museum, 1997)
Wilson D. M. *Anglo-Saxon Art* (Thames & Hudson, 1984)

Index

Earthquakes

Earthquakes

Peter Murray

THE CHILD'S WORLD®, INC.

Library of Congress Cataloging-in-Publication Data
Murray, Peter, 1952 Sept. 29–
Earthquakes / by Peter Murray.
p. cm.
Includes index.
Summary: Describes earthquakes, their causes and effects,
the instruments used to study them, and the safety
measures for preventing personal harm.
ISBN 1-56766-549-7 (library reinforced : alk paper)
1. Earthquakes—Juvenile literature.
[1. Earthquakes.] I. Title.
QE521.3.M872 1998
551.22—dc21 98-3254
CIP
AC

Photo Credits

© Andrew Rafkind/Tony Stone Worldwide: 20
© Art Gingert/Comstock, Inc.: cover
© Bruce Hands/Tony Stone Worldwide: 29
© Carl Frank, Science Source/Photo Researchers: 13
© 1991 David Olsen/Weatherstock: 26
© David Parker/Science Photo Library, Science Source/Photo Researchers: 6
© James Balog/Tony Stone Images: 15
© John Buitenkant, Science Source/Photo Researchers: 2
© Leverett Bradley/Tony Stone Images: 24
© Robert Yager/Tony Stone Images: 19
© Science Photo Library, Science Source/Photo Researchers: 9
© U.S. Geological Survey/Science Photo Library, Science Source/Photo Researchers: 23
© Van Bucher, Science Source/Photo Researchers: 10
© 1990 Warren Faidley/Weatherstock: 16
© Will & Deni McIntyre, Science Source/Photo Researchers: 30

On the cover...

Front cover: This road in Costa Rica was badly damaged by an earthquake.
Page 2: This huge crack in the ground was caused by a California earthquake.

Table of Contents

causing.

On January 17, 1994, the people of Los Angeles, California, woke up at exactly 4:31 a.m. The ground was shaking, and so were the houses and buildings. Dishes fell from cupboards, and bookcases crashed to the floor. Every car alarm in the city started howling. Gas lines and water pipes were torn open. People ran from their homes, afraid that their ceilings would collapse. What caused all of this? An earthquake!

What Is Inside Earth?

To understand earthquakes, you need to learn about Earth itself. Beneath our feet lies Earth's **crust**, a layer of cool, hard rock. It is about 60 miles thick. The crust is made up of huge pieces, or **crustal plates**. Each crustal plate is thousands of miles across. The plates fit together like pieces in a jigsaw puzzle.

The red lines in this picture show where the crustal plates fit together. ⇒

Beneath Earth's crust lies a layer of hot, melted rock called the **mantle**. The crustal plates float along on the gooey mantle, pushing against each other and pulling apart. They move so slowly that they might take a hundred years to travel an inch. Sometimes, though, they move a little faster.

What Are Earthquakes?

When crustal plates pull apart or press together, tremendous forces build up. Sometimes the plates slip and move so suddenly that we can feel the earth shift beneath our feet. When the earth moves suddenly and violently like this, we call it an earthquake.

This huge crack in Earth's crust was caused by an earthquake. ⇒

What Is a Fault?

A **fault** is a crack in the earth's crust. Most faults occur where the crustal plates meet. The *San Andreas fault* in California lies between the Pacific Ocean plate and the North American plate.

Most faults are hidden deep underground. Others lie deep under the ocean where we cannot see them. The San Andreas fault is different. It reaches all the way to Earth's surface where we can see it every day.

It is easy to see how big the San Andreas fault really is. ⇒

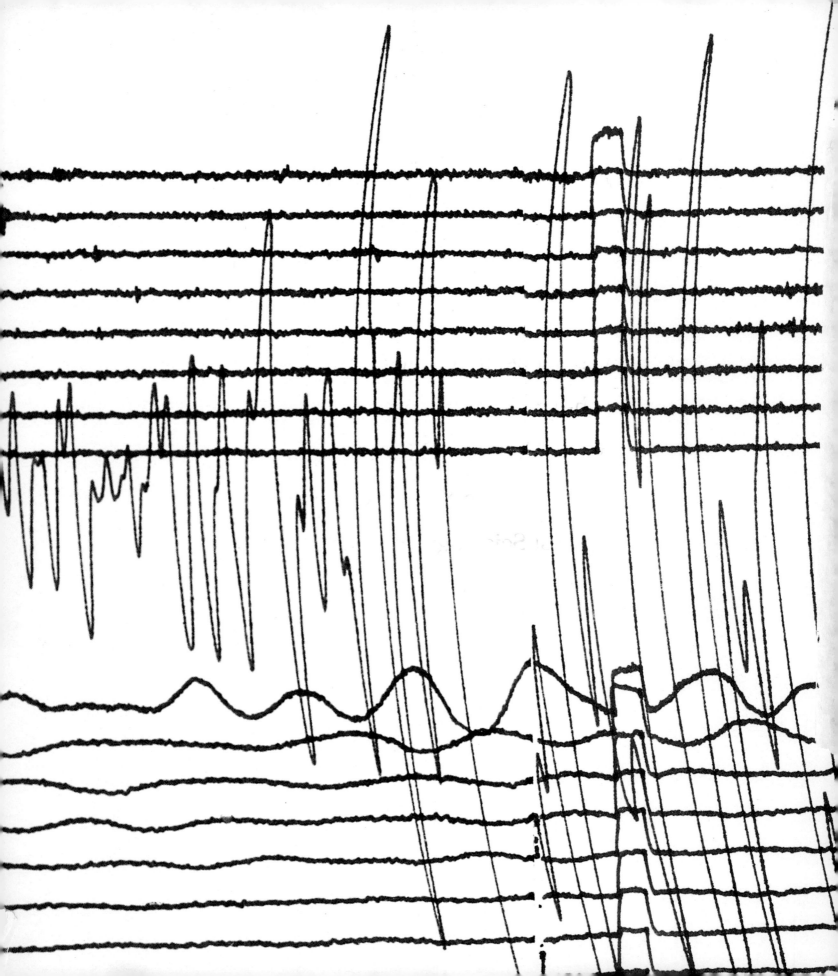

Can We Predict Earthquakes?

Scientists use machines called **seismographs** (SIZE–moh–grafs) to measure tiny movements in Earth's crust. These machines are very sensitive. In fact, a seismograph in Kansas can feel an earthquake in Los Angeles! Seismographs and other instruments help us learn more about what lies beneath our feet.

By using seismographs located in different parts of the world, scientists can tell where an earthquake started. This starting point is called the **epicenter**. Usually, the worst damage is directly above the epicenter.

In the Los Angeles earthquake of 1994, the epicenter was directly below the suburb of Northridge. Damage from the quake spread for many miles, but Northridge suffered the worst destruction. One apartment building collapsed, burying 16 people. A freeway buckled and twisted and fell apart. In nearby San Fernando, an oil pipe exploded, destroying dozens of buildings.

The 1994 earthquake badly damaged these Northridge apartments. ⇒

Do All Earthquakes Cause Damage?

Most earthquakes do little or no damage. Each year about 6,000 small earthquakes happen around the world. Luckily, only a few cause serious damage.

People who live in areas with lots of earthquakes get used to these small, harmless movements of the ground. But they never stop worrying about the big ones!

⇐ A small earthquake damaged this highway.

Can We Measure Earthquakes?

One of the strongest earthquakes ever recorded struck Anchorage, Alaska, in 1964. The Kenai Peninsula —including the entire town of Anchorage—sank seven feet. The area just to the south was raised by as much as 10 feet. The Anchorage quake measured 8.5 on the **Richter scale**. The Richter scale is a way of estimating the strength of an earthquake.

This street in Anchorage was badly damaged in the 1964 earthquake. ⇒

The weakest earthquakes we can feel measure about 2 on the Richter scale. These quakes often cause little damage. But anything over 6 is considered a strong earthquake. The Los Angeles earthquake of 1994 measured 6.5 on the Richter scale.

Can Earthquakes Cause Other Damage?

Besides destroying homes, roads, and buildings, strong earthquakes can cause other problems. They can cause avalanches and cracks in the Earth. But the deadliest effects are giant waves of water called a **tsunamis** (tsoo–NAH–meez).

Tsunamis are caused when a crustal plate beneath the ocean suddenly rises or falls. This quick movement creates enormous waves that travel up to 100 miles an hour. As tsunamis approach land, they grow larger. When the waves break onto the shore, they can destroy buildings, flood roads, and even drown people. Tsunamis are very dangerous.

⇐ Tsunamis can be even bigger than this giant wave.

What Are Some Ways to Stay Safe?

If an earthquake strikes, the first thing you should do is go outside. Outside, there are fewer things that could fall on you, such as bookshelves, windows, or walls. Go to an open area and stay there. Watch out for fallen power lines and broken glass. When the shaking stops, don't go back inside! Earthquakes are often followed by smaller quakes called *aftershocks*. Aftershocks can cause weakened buildings to collapse.

Poles are keeping this building from falling down during aftershocks. ⇒

In California people talk about "The Big One." The Big One is an earthquake that hasn't happened yet. It's the earthquake everyone fears will happen when forces building along the San Andreas fault suddenly give way.

No one knows for sure what the future will bring. There may not be another major earthquake for years—or the Big One might happen tomorrow! Scientists are watching their seismographs very closely. They hope that some day, they will be able to warn people before dangerous earthquakes occur.

⇐ A strong California earthquake did this damage in 1989.

Glossary

crust (KRUST)
The outer shell of Earth is called the crust. Earth's crust is about 60 miles thick.

crustal plates (KRUS–tull PLAYTS)
The huge sections of the Earth's crust are called crustal plates. The crustal plates fit together like a jigsaw puzzle.

epicenter (EH–pih–sen–ter)
The epicenter of an earthquake is the place where the quake started. The worst damage usually occurs at the epicenter.

fault (FALT)
A fault is a crack in Earth's crust. The San Andreas fault is a huge fault in California.

mantle (MAN–tull)
The mantle is a layer of hot, melted rock underneath Earth's crust. The crustal plates float on the mantle.

seismographs (SIZE–moh–grafs)
Seismographs are machines that detect and measure tiny movements of Earth's crust.

Richter scale (RIK–ter SKAYL)
The Richter scale is a way of estimating how strong an earthquake is.

tsunamis (tsoo–NAH–meez)
Tsunamis are huge waves that are created by earthquakes. Tsunamis can be very destructive.

Index